Book *illegible*

Page 61

AWAKE AT THE WHEEL

George ohsawa

=> Zen Macrobiotics

↓

E+ewhon

One Peaceful World

Awake at the *Wheel*

Norio Kushi's Highway Adventures and
the Unmasking of the Phantom Self

Stephen Earle

Foreword by Norio Kushi

TAT Foundation Press

Published by TAT Foundation Press
Thomas Green Road
Roxboro, North Carolina 27574
Tatfoundation.org

Cover design by Ward Saunders
Text font: Baskerville
Main entry under title: *Awake at the Wheel*

1. Spirituality 2. Psychology

ISBN: 978-0-9864457-3-6

Library of Congress Control Number: 2018951083

Table of Contents

Foreword

IN 2004, PURELY OUT OF curiosity, I embarked upon an inquiry into what it is to be human. Little did I know this inquiry would result in the shattering of the fundamental ideas I, like everyone, held as to who—or rather, *what*—we are as human beings.

A year into looking at the world through the lens of "What does it mean to be human?" I was hit over the head with the cosmic two-by-four. What I saw, I now refer to as the human dilemma: that we don't know what we are, and we don't know that we don't know. This is the dilemma that we as humanity find ourselves in today. We never question our fundamental beliefs about our world, beginning with everything and anything we think the "I" in "I am" is.

We all have our beliefs and positions, some of which are inherited and others, self-cultivated. It's not my purpose to challenge such beliefs or positions.

Rather, what is being offered here is an invitation to look at how one can discover for oneself the magic and beauty of *how* our reality is created. The challenge for me, ever since being hit over the head with the cosmic two-by-four, has been to articulate and describe this way of inquiry in a way that is useful to others.

Enter long-time friend Stephen Earle. Steve and I met casually in the late-1960s, then spent time together in Japan in 1973 and 1974. We've since remained in contact, and we've shared an interest in understanding what place each of us occupies in the cosmos. Our differing personalities have brought us along different paths, but our conversations over the years have continued to focus on our common existential curiosity.

Steve, along his path, came to an understanding of the role of language in what we are as humans in a way I had never considered. Along with this, Steve has developed writing skills best described as artistic.

Enter Abby Murphy, who has delved into many teachings and studied with a number of teachers, both in this country and in India. More importantly, as Steve and I delightfully discovered, she is a perceptive and insightful editor.

I am grateful to both Steve and Abby for their collaboration, the result of which is the book you are now holding. The pages that follow tell the story of someone named Norio. The point in telling this story is to share "how to see" past our inherited ways of thinking and to see the infinite core of our true nature, out of which our beliefs, positions and ideologies are created. This book is not about ideas, nor is it about improving or fixing anyone or anything. It is simply an invitation to join one another as one would join a group of friends walking through a forest, and then, with childlike curiosity, to see together what we can see.

Thank you for reading this book.

Norio Kushi

Introduction

To say life is a journey is to tire an already tired metaphor, but it nevertheless rings true. Who among us as children could have predicted the life we are living today? And who among us can say with absolute certainty what is going to happen tomorrow? Moreover, would any one of us have it any other way? Uncertainty is the spice of life; it's that which generates its adventures, its challenges, its joys and sorrows.

For Norio Kushi, the journey is also his livelihood. Norio drives a truck. He has been driving commercially—taxis, buses, trucks—for over forty years, and today, at the age of sixty-three, he continues to log upwards of 140,000 miles a year traveling back and forth across the continental United States.

This book is the story of Norio's journey, how he was born in New York City to Japanese parents, how he grew up and came of age within the eccentric surroundings of the Boston macrobiotic community of the 1960s and 1970s, and how, since then, he has consistently been guided by his intuition. It is also the story of how he discovered life's single most overarching principle—that it's not going to turn out!—and how he also discovered that the driver of the truck was not who he thought it was.

My friendship with Norio begin in 1973 when I was in my early twenties, he in his late teens, and both of us living in Japan. He is the oldest son of Michio and Aveline Kushi, inspirational teachers of macrobiotics and pioneers of the natural and organic foods movement who were also, incidentally, persons of singular influence upon my life story, particularly as it was out of my exposure to their teachings that I developed my life-long passion for and association with Japan and things Japanese. While our life paths differ, Norio's and mine have crossed countless times over the years; we have tracked each other's movements and growth and have laughed together along the way about our respective successes and unseemly failures. When I settled in Richmond, Virginia and he, later, in Asheville, North Carolina, and after he returned to truck driving in 2002, I would occasionally return home from work to find an eighteen-wheeler parked on our street and know that Norio had dropped by to visit.

In 2005, something changed. Norio began communicating via email, telephone, or during his occasional visits about a series of, call them realizations or revelations he had had while driving in California. This was unlike Norio; our conversations up until then had always revolved around the mundane—family, friends, work, mutual interests, and so on. Neither I nor others I knew who were also communicating with him could quite make sense of what he was saying, partly because of the limits of Norio's powers of self-expression but mostly because of the evident ineffability of what he was trying to describe. But regardless of whether what he was saying made sense, immediately evident to all was that he also emanated a new kind of presence. Norio was still Norio; the personality we were familiar with was still there. However, behind that personality was now an unwavering equanimity we hadn't seen before. There was a sense of someone fully present to life as it unfolded and capable of accepting whatever it brought his way.

Since then, Norio's powers of articulation and description have improved. That improvement has come through practice, as more and more opportunities and venues have opened for him to tell his story and to deliver the punchline to what he refers to as the cosmic joke—that everything we think we are is a fiction and that the only thing between us and fulfillment is ourselves.

Audiences, however, have finite attention spans, and talks are subject to the restraints of time and place. He and I have been talking for years about the need for a book that expands upon his insights and can reach more people. At first, I encouraged him to write it, promising to help with the final product. Eventually, we both realized this was not going to happen, and the thrust of our discussion turned toward Norio providing the material and me doing the writing. At the time, however, I was immersed in another writing project, a historical biography set in early and mid-twentieth century Japan that involved substantial research. Thus preoccupied, I found it difficult to shift my attention to Norio's story for long enough to do it justice.

This changed after *Heaven's Wind: The Life and Teachings of Nakamura Tempu* was published in April 2017. Norio and I resumed our discussions, I accompanied him to a weekend workshop he led in Philadelphia, and quite suddenly this book began falling into place.

Norio and I express ourselves differently, and by mutual consent he is not listed as co-author because the writing is distinctively mine. That said, I have endeavored to be factually accurate and to stay on message consistent with his descriptions of the events, as well as their interior dimensions, and he has corrected me when wrong and elaborated when my understanding has been too narrow or shallow. As collaborations go, it has been a good one, and to take Norio at his word, we are both pleased with the result.

Norio's insights, the windfall of long hours on the road, are the stuff of practical wisdom. Be advised that you read this book at your own risk: chances are, it will at least challenge your conceptual understanding of reality and may even alter forever how you see the world. But the ability to question one's reality, he and I would argue, is the first requisite of evolutionary change. Awakening—you might also call it spiritual transformation or enlightenment—is neither a solution to life's problems nor a goal to be achieved through personal endeavor but, rather, a ground zero, a place to come from if one is to live a productive and fulfilling life.

More importantly, this book argues, individual acquaintance with that ground zero is essential to the future of human social growth and development. We live in an age beset by imponderable problems—impending ecological disaster, extremely tenuous financial stability, and deteriorating international relations, to name but a few. What stands out about these problems is both their immediacy and their complexity; there are no easy solutions. That said, what should also be self-evident to anyone attracted to this book is that almost all these problems are ultimately symptoms of infantile and adolescent human behavior, and consequently, practical remedies alone are necessary but insufficient to their solution. What is most needed is an evolutionary shift toward human maturity. Luckily, that does not mean the bulk of humanity needs to make that shift—if that were the case we would surely be doomed. Rather, the movement of some minimal mass of individuals to the vanguard of human development may be enough to tip the scales. The point, however, is that such maturity cannot come about absent some recognition on the part of individuals as to just who or what we are.

For that reason and that reason alone, Norio's story is important. His journey is not one that points toward a destination but, instead, one that questions the nature of who it is that sits in the driver's seat. If you come away from this book with more questions than answers, we will be rewarded, and our endeavor, a success.

Acknowledgements

As INDICATED BY NORIO IN his foreword, the making of this book involved a third collaborator whose name does not appear on the cover. Abby Murphy was the sounding board for everything written. She challenged me whenever my writing was less than spot-on, and she took me to task every time I misplaced a comma. The finished work reflects both her vigilance and her good humor.

Denny and Susan Waxman hosted Norio for a weekend-long seminar in June 2017 and graciously invited me to accompany him. This event proved to be the catalyst out of which this book began to take form.

Heather Lacey contributed recordings of her telephone conversations with Norio. Kinloch Earle and Lianna Kushi read drafts of *Awake at the Wheel* and provided comments. James Silver served as a sounding board for my description of the Boston macrobiotic community of the 1960s and 1970s.

While Norio nonsense is the focus of this book, inevitably, a fair amount of Steve nonsense has made its way into the pages. I would be remiss were I not to credit the three teachers who have most influenced my worldview. They are, in chronological order, Norio's father, Michio Kushi, to whom I owe my good health, my enduring fascination with Japanese culture, and my first exposure to holistic thinking; Odano Sanae, whose twenty-three years of spiritual mentorship opened my eyes to the miracle that is language; and Ken Wilber, from whose books and talks I have taken away an understanding of reality as a multi-perspectival and developmentally differentiated affair.

Norio and I are grateful to Shawn Nevins and the TAT Foundation for their willingness to put this book into print. TAT is making an invaluable contribution to the conversation surrounding spiritual growth, and we are delighted to be associated with them.

Friend and local Richmond artist Ward Saunders contributed his time and talent to produce a cover that provides a worthy window into the book's content.

Norio thanks JoAnne and I thank Akemi for putting up with our respective nonsense for all these years.

1

THE TIME JOHN LENNON CAME TO VISIT

NORIO KUSHI, AGE FIVE, IS sitting on a park bench with his mother, Aveline Kushi, in Flushing Meadows, Queens, New York. He is munching on the picnic lunch she has packed, and she is nursing his infant brother Phiya.

"Always trust your feelings," she says. "Feelings are what will guide you through life."

She is speaking in Japanese, and Norio doesn't fully understand the words she uses—nor does he remember them today. But he understands their intent. In the immediate way that a child absorbs his mother's world, he knows exactly what she means, and he imbibes her advice whole and without question.

Young Norio can't describe the feeling Aveline is referring to, but he knows it as not just any kind of feeling. It's special. It arises within the body as a pulse- or wave-like sensation that permeates the cells of every tissue and organ. And when it arises, the mind goes quiet.

It also occurs outside of normal time. The entire process—the feeling—has a beginning, middle, and end, but it nevertheless occurs all at once. The qualities of that timeless instant are clarity and prescience.

Prescient clarity may give rise to an image or thought, and when it does, the image or thought is recognized as a vision, directive, or insight. It is also recognized not as a possibility or probability but as a fact. Even when it invokes a future event, that future is already so, such that the question of whether the feeling is to be trusted never even comes up.

Anytime his mother goes out, Norio is quick to jump in the car. He is all about moving vehicles, a passion his siblings don't share; they are more content to stay home. Today he has ridden with his mother to a carpet store on Roosevelt Avenue in Jackson Heights, and she is looking at carpets with the store proprietor at her side. The car ride finished, Norio is bored. But there is a train stop nearby. He asks his mother for fifteen cents so he can go ride the trains. He will meet her back at the house, he promises.

Riding the trains is a favorite hobby. Eight years old now, he sometimes travels from Flushing to lower Manhattan and back on his own. Furthermore, Aveline tolerates this hobby; she has confidence in his sense of direction, which she also recognizes as far superior to her own. She gives him the fifteen cents, and he runs up the steps to the elevated station over Roosevelt Avenue.

The Long Island trains are new to him; this is the Flushing line, and he has never ridden it before. But undaunted, he hops aboard and rides several stops. Then, on impulse, he gets off at Willets Point. Not that he knows Willets Point, but something tells him it shouldn't be far from home.

Emerging onto the street, he finds himself in unfamiliar surroundings. The station stands at an intersection with streets going off in four directions. With no clue as to which way to go, he looks for someone to ask—a policeman, perhaps—but the streets are deserted.

Little Norio looks down each street in turn, wondering which he should take. And when none of them suggests itself to him, he looks again. One by one, he peers as far down each street as he can see. Only after this second pass does he realize, "I'm lost."

It's a simple admission, to which he attaches neither anguish nor dread; he is just acknowledging what is so. But with that admission, something shifts. His young mind takes in that the problem is not one it can work out. No amount of deductive reasoning is going to show him the way home, and consequently, he stops trying. His mind goes quiet.

Just then he has the feeling. And with the feeling comes certainty. He now knows exactly which street he is to take. No longer lost, he sets off in the direction of home.

Norio walks for what feels like an hour through unfamiliar neighborhoods, never once doubting he is going in the right direction. Until, finally, he comes to an overpass that looks down on the Long Island Expressway. This is home turf. He has ridden his bicycle out to this overpass many times to hang on the railing and watch the traffic pass below. From here, it's an easy two-mile walk to his door.

His mother greets him cheerfully when he enters. "Okaeri-nasai," she says in Japanese. "Welcome home."

The Beatles are coming! It's August 1966, and the Kushis are now living in Brookline, Massachusetts. Norio's father and mother are teaching macrobiotics, a practical philosophy of health and wellness based on principles of oriental medicine and a whole-foods-based diet, and their house is one of several "study houses" in Brookline and Cambridge that takes in students, predominantly in their twenties, as boarders.

The Kushis currently have some fifteen of these young men and women living with them, and the house is abuzz. The Beatles are to perform at Suffolk Downs on August 18, and several of the boarders have secured tickets. Norio wants to join them. More than anything else, he wants to see the Beatles.

But this time, Aveline is putting her foot down. A rock-and-roll concert is no place for an eleven-year-old boy. Her answer is a simple "No."

They are seated at the kitchen table. His mother just doesn't understand. She doesn't see the importance of the occasion. How can he explain? He begs, and he pleads.

Aveline looks him in the eye. "They will be back again," she says. "You can see them next time."

Norio goes suddenly quiet. He is thinking about what she has just said. Then he answers. "No, they won't. They won't be back."

He is, of course, right. But no one—not even the Beatles themselves—knows it yet. The decision is made after their return to London at the end of the month. They are, they announce, giving up touring and will concentrate solely on recording; the 1966 U.S. tour was their last.

Norio doesn't know how he knows, but he knows. The Beatles will not be back. And this makes it all the more imperative he attend the concert.

"Mom," he pleads. "This is going to be the last chance. I have to see the Beatles!"

Aveline will not be swayed. His supplications are having no effect.

At last he gets it. It's useless to argue; she isn't going to change her mind. He has lost. He isn't going to see the Beatles. Not gonna happen.

In that moment, he has that special feeling again. He goes quiet and listens.

"Mom," he says suddenly. "John Lennon is coming to visit us."

"Who is John Lennon?" she asks.

"One of the Beatles!"

"Oh! Well, that will be nice."

With that, Norio is satisfied. No more need to see the Beatles at Suffolk Downs, because one of the Beatles, his favorite one, is coming to visit! He slides out of his chair and runs outside to play. The entire matter thus put to rest, he thinks no more about the concert. He also thinks no more about John Lennon's impending visit or questions when it might occur.

Ten years and one month later, on Thursday, September 16, 1976, Norio—who now supports himself by driving a taxi—pulls into a downtown Boston taxi stand, hops out, and climbs into the passenger seat of the cab in front of him. Behind the wheel is a fellow cabbie named Doug.

"Hey Doug, how's it going?"

Doug's face is buried in the Boston Globe. "How 'bout this," he says without looking up. "It says John Lennon is in Boston."

"Show it to me!" Norio says. He takes the paper out of Doug's hands. Sure enough, on the second page in the bottom right corner is a one-paragraph insertion under the headline "A Beatle in Boston." It says only that John Lennon and Yoko Ono have just arrived in Boston, are staying at the Copley Plaza Hotel, and plan to visit friends in Brookline.

"I've got to get home," Norio exclaims. He exits Doug's cab and jumps back into his own. Taking Beacon Street to Brookline and then maneuvering side streets he knows like the back of his hand, he pulls into the yard of the Kushis' house on Buckminster Road. He calls to his mother as he runs inside. "Mom! John Lennon is finally coming to visit!"

It's the middle of the day, and the house is quiet. Norio's father and siblings, as well as the boarders, are out. But Aveline is home and emerges from the room she uses as her office. By now, she knows perfectly well who John Lennon is and listens with mild surprise as Norio tells her about the paragraph in the Boston Globe.

Just then, the telephone rings. Aveline answers. And from her reaction, he knows. John Lennon is on the line.

The following day, an unostentatious green Chrysler Town & Country station wagon with faux-wood side panels pulls into the driveway. Out pile John, Yoko, their young son Sean, Sean's Japanese nanny, and their chauffeur, also Japanese. Michio and Aveline usher them into the living room.

John's explanation of how it is they have come to be visiting the Kushis puts an ordinary face on the event. Several days earlier, he and Yoko had lunched with friends, author William Dufty (*Lady Sings the Blues*, his 1956 biography of Billie Holliday; *Sugar Blues*, 1975; and *Swanson on Swanson*, 1980) and his wife, actress

Gloria Swanson (star of silent film and the 1950 classic *Sunset Boulevard*). Bill and Gloria mentioned they were planning to visit the Kushi household in Brookline that coming Friday. Long-time friends of the Kushis, they had held their wedding ceremony—dressed in kimonos—in the Kushis' living room one year earlier, and this time, they would be commemorating their anniversary.

John and Yoko subsequently hatched a scheme. They would surprise Bill and Gloria by showing up at the Kushi residence for the occasion. Only when John called ahead from their hotel—the phone call taken by Aveline—did he learn that Bill and Gloria had had a last-minute change of plans and had stayed in New York. But Aveline was quick to insist they come anyway, and John and Yoko, who were practicing macrobiotics and eager to meet Michio and Aveline, gladly accepted.

Throughout his life, Norio has continued to be informed and guided by his feelings, especially that special feeling with its accompanying certainty. In a pivotal moment in his journey at age forty-seven, he realized, based on that feeling, that "Life is not going to turn out." Also based on that feeling, he went back to making his living by driving a truck.

2

THE END OF LIVING
FOR A FUTURE

IT IS SEPTEMBER 2002, AND Norio is living in Asheville,
North Carolina. He and his wife JoAnne have just been
talking. Now he is alone, standing in the kitchen.

Norio and JoAnne moved to Asheville with their
five children three years ago so that he could manage
a small, natural and macrobiotic foods mail order
and distribution company on behalf of the business's
absentee owner, a good friend. To his and his friend's
chagrin, that business has now gone under, and he has
spent the last weeks liquidating its few remaining assets
and tying up loose ends. Out of work, the foremost

question on his mind, as well as JoAnne's, is, what is he going to do?

At forty-seven, he has a high school education and a less-than-compelling work history; most of his professional life has been spent driving either taxis, trucks, or buses. Nor is this recent business debacle going to help him in the job market. Resumes are out to potential employers, but by conventional standards, truth be told, he is eminently unemployable. What's more, JoAnne wants a separation.

The state of his marriage aside, he has his children to think about—including, in addition to the five in Asheville, another from a prior relationship. Of course, he will provide for them; that is a given. But how? What will he do?

How has he managed to make such a mess of things? And how is he going to make them right again?

These are the thoughts swirling in his head as he stands in the kitchen. But the problems confronting him, he also sees, are not to be solved by mulling over options. The situation is demanding of action, and he is short of ideas. It's in that moment that the nature of the impasse he is up against reveals itself in scale. It's insurmountable. That is, his mental faculties, he recognizes, are incapable of delivering real answers; he is never going to figure out what he should do. And because his mind sees that it can't possibly think its way out of the predicament it finds itself in, it hits a wall.

He pauses. He looks out the window. His attention is drawn to the leaves of the trees, still green and blowing gently in the early autumn wind. This is when it comes to him. It comes to him verbally. "Life is not going to turn out."

So obvious, so simple. He has, he sees, been living for a future. He has been living as though his current existence is just a transitory phase, as though life would inevitably turn out to be as it is supposed to be and his problems will all find their solutions.

Above all, he has been living for success. He has even given that success a number: fifteen million dollars. When he has money, he will also have a large house with several fast, shiny automobiles in the garage. He will be surrounded by family and friends. Life will be good. It will be complete.

But now, with the same sort of clarity and certainty with which, at age eleven, he had pictured John Lennon sitting in his family's living room, he sees there is no such thing as a future state of completion. Life is just one thing after another. How shallow of him to have invested in a belief to the contrary. Life is not going to turn out because life doesn't occur in the future; it occurs right now.

Much later, when Norio tells others about this realization, he is surprised to find they hear it as either a statement of resignation or an admission of defeat. But such was not the case. Rather, the realization that life isn't going to turn out was liberating. It allows him to walk away from all the hopes and expectations he had placed on life, and he feels as though an enormous weight has been lifted from his shoulders. He is done, once and for all, with success and failure. The slate has been wiped clean. All that is left is what is, here and now. *Success and failure are not in your hands.*

Moreover, in the context of here and now, his priorities are eminently clear. Whereas before, the notion of livelihood and providing for family had been tangled up with his sense of self-worth, now, since success is no longer at stake, self-worth is not even an issue. What remains is his responsibility to his family, and this he accepts freely and wholeheartedly.

The fuller implications of what has just happened only become evident to Norio over time. The shift away from living for a future, he discovers, belongs not to this one occasion. It is permanent. Because once the mind fully sees its projection of the future as an unexamined and utterly ineffective strategy for dealing with the present, it stops projecting. And because it no longer

Don't be in a future driven way of living

projects, it also never looks back. Never is he to return to his former, future-driven way of being.

Furthermore, what also ends with the realization that life isn't going to turn out is his consternation over what to do next. He no longer faces decisions; the answer to "What next?" is always obvious. Choice, he understands, isn't made between alternatives. Rather, in the same way that he has chosen to provide for his family, choice shows up as the willful acceptance of what is so. Or, one might say, alternatives have a way of collapsing into a single imperative before they even enter one's awareness.

Such is the case right now, for he now knows how he is going to earn a living. He goes back into the dining room where JoAnne is still sitting and says to her, "I know what I'll do. I'll drive a truck."

Arnold Norio Kushi was born in Manhattan on December 15, 1954, the Kushi's second child and the first of their four sons. His fascination for things that go vroom vroom began almost as soon as he could walk.

During his early years, all spent in Queens—first Rego Park and then Flushing—his attention drifted naturally to the city trains, the traffic on the Long Island Expressway, and his bicycle. Then, in March 1964, on a whim, Aveline moved the family to Martha's Vineyard

(Michio stayed behind to continue his work in the city for Takashimaya, a prestigious Japanese department store). Norio recalls careening down the highway, he and his siblings packed into a '63 Plymouth Belvedere station wagon with his mother at the wheel and a trailer hitched behind.

The car began swaying from side to side, and Aveline exclaimed, "Anbalance, anbalance!" Norio looked to the front and the rear but saw no sign of an ambulance. Then he realized what she was saying. It was "Unbalanced, unbalanced!"

They stopped at a service area. Also riding with them was the first of the Kushis' live-in students, Robert Fulton, and now he assumed the wheel. He drove them to Woods Hole, where they boarded the car onto the Islander ferry and crossed to Vineyard Haven. Then he drove again, delivering them finally to Gay Head on the island's far western tip and the house they would call home for the next six months.

Norio was fascinated with the Belvedere. It was a cantankerous machine, beleaguered by frequent breakdowns. One morning, Aveline went out the door to run an errand in Vineyard Haven, and Norio, as usual, was quick to follow. He climbed into the passenger seat. But when Aveline turned the key, nothing happened. The car wouldn't start.

Fulton was the Kushis' go-to-guy in residence for dealing with the Belvedere's quirks. His father, also named Robert (and yes, a direct descendant of the inventor of the steamboat that first sailed the Hudson in 1807), was an accomplished inventor and mechanical engineer. So, when Aveline called for him, young Robert came out and gave it a try. No success. The engine would not turn over.

Watching all this from the passenger seat, Norio had another of his moments of clarity. "I can start the car!" he told them. He was certain, even though he had never once started a car before.

His impassioned plea, however, failed to elicit a response from either Fulton or his mother. Perhaps they didn't hear.

"Mom, I can start the car!" he insisted a second time.

His mother's glance made it clear this was not the time for the clamoring of a nine-year-old boy. Not until Fulton went back into the house to call a wrecker, leaving them with nothing to do but wait, did she give him his chance. She handed him the key.

Norio slid over into the driver's seat, put the key in the ignition, and turned it. The car started right up.

The quiet roads of Martha's Vineyard were perfect for a boy on his bike. Over the course of the summer, Norio rode the forty-some mile island circuit many times.

He also got it into his head that he wanted to fly in an airplane. In early June, he talked his mother into buying him a one-way airline ticket from Martha's Vineyard to New York. Aveline took him to the airport, and Norio flew the short hop to La Guardia on a twin prop DC-3 with an unpressurized cabin. As the plane rose to its cruising elevation of barely seven thousand feet, he marveled at the view of Long Island Sound.

His mother, who was incapable of worry, had made no arrangements for him at the other end. Not that arrangements were necessary, for he knew exactly what to do. He caught a bus into Manhattan and then took the subway several stops to a station connecting him with the F Train to Flushing. Once in Flushing, he showed up at the door of family friends named Nakamura.

In September, the Kushis moved again, this time to Cambridge, Massachusetts. Michio had concluded his responsibilities at Takashimaya and was now devoting himself fulltime to teaching macrobiotics.

Norio soon began cycling from Cambridge to Wellesley and back, twenty miles each way, to visit a friend. And when the family moved yet again in March

1966 from Cambridge to Brookline, he extended his reach twenty miles west to Framingham and sixty miles north to Gloucester. The following year, he added Cape Cod and Martha's Vineyard to his route, sometimes cycling from Brookline to Cape Cod and back, about one hundred and fifty miles, all in the same day.

"Wouldn't it be fun," he thought to himself, "to ride my bike across a national border?" After a week of persistent cajoling, he persuaded friend Steven Finley to buy into the scheme, and somehow the two of them negotiated respective parental consent. In the summer of 1969, Norio and Steve, both age fourteen, bicycled from Brookline to Montreal. It took them four days.

On their return, in Northern Vermont, they came to a long hill. Steve had ridden ahead and was out of sight when Norio doggedly began the climb. It was midday and excruciatingly hot. In the heat, the hill seemed interminable.

Their route was different from the one they had taken on their way up to Montreal, but from his map, Norio knew just where they were. They were cycling east on route 302, approaching East Barre. In East Barre, they would turn right onto route 110 and head south.

The hill, he told himself, would surely crest at this junction. From there, they would either be on the level or coasting downhill. "I just need to get to the top of this hill," he thought. But, upon arriving at East Barre and turning onto route 110, he found himself looking up a hill even longer than the one he had just climbed.

Norio didn't stop. He was not going to be defeated by a hill, and whether he had it in him to keep going was not the issue. It was the heat. The hill was long but climbable; the heat, however, was almost intolerable. He just continued to push down on the pedals, one at a time, all the while wrestling with the oppressive heat.

At last, he came to the top of the hill. He coasted into the lot of a small gas station, put a dime in the soft drink machine, and bought a bottle of Fanta. Then he sat in the shade by the side of the road. It was still hot, but here at the top of the hill there was a slight breeze. The Fanta was cooling to his hands and even more cooling and refreshing as it slid down his throat. It was sweet relief, and he was satisfied and at peace with the world.

Then a curious thought percolated into his awareness. "What," he wondered, "is it that has changed?" The difference between how the world had looked as he struggled up the hill and how it looked now as he sipped his bottle of Fanta was striking. "What is it that makes the difference?"

Insight answered. His discomfort on the hill had been a product of neither the heat nor the length of the climb. It had been a product of the way he was talking to himself about the heat and the climb. The problem was so obvious and the solution so simple: talking to himself about the heat served no purpose other than to make him uncomfortable; all he needed to do was to stop the talk.

This he did for the rest of the journey. Furthermore, the habit stuck. From that moment to the present, no matter how hot the weather, Norio says, heat has never bothered him. It was his first recognition of the immediacy with which thought affects the quality of experience and a harbinger of things to come.

Norio and Steve continued to ride together in subsequent years, even after Steve went off to college and then into business. Their crowning achievement came in 1978, when Norio, now twenty-four, saved up enough from his earnings as a cabbie to take a couple of months off during the summer. He and Steve traveled with their bicycles by train to Jasper, Alberta, Canada, and cycled south, crisscrossing the Great Divide. They cycled through Glacier National park and Missoula, Montana. They cycled through Yellowstone to Jackson Hole, then into Colorado, continuing all the way south to Durango. From there, they headed west, through Canyonlands, Bryce, and Zion National Parks to Las Vegas and on to California. Heading north, they climbed through the Sierra Nevadas to the Cascade Range, passing through Klamath Falls, Oregon, and Yakima, Washington, before arriving finally in Seattle. In just under six weeks they had bicycled over four thousand miles.

In Big Pine, California, after a grueling ride across Death Valley where the temperature was 120 degrees, Norio got sick. He was running a fever and eliminating from both ends. Nevertheless, he persevered. The fever made him delirious, and to this day his memory of the trip after Big Pine is spotty. He managed the climb over Tioga Pass into Yosemite but forewent the one to Crater Lake in Oregon, a spot he had been eager to visit. Upon reaching Seattle, he collapsed in the care of friends and remained bedridden for a month.

Steve Finley pursued a career in biochemistry, first contributing to the early growth of biotech innovator Amgen and then co-founding PeproTech. He died in 2003 when the bush plane he was piloting, no passengers aboard, went down off the coast of Alaska.

When, at sixteen, Norio drove away from his driving test, license in hand, he didn't stop. He drove first to

New York, then to Philadelphia, and then to Pittsburgh, Indianapolis, Ann Arbor, Toronto, and Niagara Falls before returning home to Brookline.

He was already an experienced driver. Since the age of twelve he had ridden back and forth across the country—to and from Los Angeles and Seattle—about ten times in vehicles owned and operated by various macrobiotic community members, and these people, upon discovering his passion for driving, gladly let him spell them for long sections of highway. Back in Brookline, a girlfriend parked her Triumph for several months in the Kushis' driveway and left Norio with the keys while she went off to California. He drove the car freely around the city for the duration. Massachusetts required he take Driver's Ed—it was either that or wait until his seventeenth birthday—before he tested for his license, so he commuted to Driver's Ed in the Triumph, parking it just around the corner.

He had also already dropped out of school. The summer before his sophomore year in high school, Aveline, with the Kushi children in tow, moved temporarily to California to manage a macrobiotic study house in Hollywood. Norio started at Hollywood High but didn't like it. He then migrated on his own to Seattle, where he stayed with friends and attended a Seattle high school for several months. Weeks before the school year ended, however, he lost all interest and stayed away.

Back in Hollywood the following fall, he enrolled in Fairfax High. He had been attending for about a month when, one morning, he walked into school, stopped, and looked around. It was a morning like every other. Students were arriving, visiting their lockers, jostling and carrying on in the halls, and then dispersing to their respective classes; and teachers, class materials in hand, were likewise making their way to their classrooms.

"Something is wrong with this picture," Norio thought to himself. He turned around, walked home, and never looked back. What exactly had been wrong with the picture, he couldn't say; he only knew he didn't belong in it. "I'm done with school," he informed his mother. Aveline accepted this news without objection. Later when he told his father, Michio's only comment was, "Don't waste your life."

Freed from the classroom, he sought new experiences. Foremost among his interests were girls. His first romantic encounter at fifteen, with a girl one year younger than he, was abruptly terminated when the girl's parents found out the two were sexually involved; she was barred from seeing him again. Norio, genuinely in love, was crushed. He decided to pursue older women whose parents would not be a problem.

His next girlfriend was thirteen years his senior; the next, eleven.

Much to his parents' distress, he also experimented with marijuana. "It spaced me out too much," he says. "After one high, I wouldn't feel normal for three days. For me, normal was the feeling I could hop on my bicycle at a moment's notice and ride 100 miles."

In late 1972, he set off for Japan. The Vietnam War was still raging, and he wanted to put distance between himself and his draft board. The decision, however, also received parental blessing; Michio and Aveline were hopeful that a closer association with his ancestral heritage might help to straighten him out. He crossed the Pacific aboard a passenger freighter called the Brazil Maru, a sixteen-day voyage that turned out also to be the Brazil Maru's last, and stayed with his grandparents in Tokyo. After six months, he moved on, first to Kyoto, where he roomed next door to Michio and Aveline's good friends the Yamaguchis, and then to Osaka, where he washed dishes in the back of a small macrobiotic restaurant. His stay in Japan lasted two years.

Back in Boston, Norio secured his taxi operator's license. For most of the remainder of the seventies, except for a short stint on the peanut butter manufacturing line in the South Boston warehouse of Erewhon, the Kushis' burgeoning natural foods company, he drove a cab in and around Boston. Also during this time, through a chance encounter on the subway, he was invited to assist with public transportation studies being conducted for the Massachusetts Transit Authority and Logan Airport.

In 1980, he received his trucker's license and began taking part-time work as a delivery driver, and by the following year this had become fulltime. In 1983, he moved to Fairfield, Connecticut, to drive for Chestnut Hill Bus, beginning an eleven-year association with the New England bus industry. After he and JoAnne were married, they lived in Burlington, Vermont, where Norio first drove a tractor-trailer for UPS. But when they found out JoAnne was pregnant with their first child, he secured a job in sales for a local bus company, allowing him to stay closer to home.

The company operated both regular bus routes and charter services, and Norio secured a lucrative book of repeat charter business originating out of Japan. The bus industry, however, was already in a state of decline, and restructuring and consolidation were rampant. Norio moved between companies and worked in various capacities, including management. By this time, he knew the industry and all its players, from management to station managers, dispatchers, and drivers, and as part of a new startup, he was instrumental in putting together a successful bid for a large contract with Amtrak.

Meanwhile, his father's work had entered a new stage. Michio was lecturing not only throughout the U.S. but also in Europe, Latin America, and Japan. Charismatic and inspiring in front of audiences, he had become, internationally, the figurehead for the macrobiotic movement.

But he was also ambitious, and his ambitions had a way of going awry when they mixed with business. From time to time, Norio's father and mother would entice Norio back to help with various ill-conceived schemes, and each time, in the inevitable aftermath, he swore, "Never again." At their insistence, he oversaw the planning and buildout of a macrobiotic Japanese restaurant in Stockbridge, Massachusetts, having been promised that the money needed to finance the project would be there. It wasn't. The restaurant was forced to open in a state of semi-completion and then to close soon after.

Another time, his father lured him into a startup that was to mass market natural foods under the Kushi name. The venture was to be capitalized through a public offering on the NASDAQ. The people who had come to his father with this scheme evidently knew a lot about the stock market, but they knew nothing about the retail food industry. Norio witnessed gross mismanagement at close hand and warned his father. But Michio would not be moved. Each time Norio spoke to him, he reaffirmed his faith in his Wall Street guys. Within less than two years, the company was auctioned off as a shell for pennies on the dollar.

These years also brought tragedy to the Kushis. In 1992 Aveline and Lily, Norio's older sister, were both diagnosed with cervical cancer. Lily died in 1995 at the age of forty-one. Aveline passed away six years later in 2001, at the age of 78.

When, in August 1999, a friend in Japan, a businessman who had acquired a small distributer and mail order retailer of macrobiotic foods in Asheville, North Carolina, offered him the management of the company, Norio took it. He had been in and around the natural food industry since childhood, and he wanted to try his hand at business free of his father's oversight. But the company, he soon discovered, had been plundered of most of its assets by his friend's minority American partner. He helped his friend through the pain and acrimony associated with getting rid of the partner and then began to pick up the pieces.

The company turned out to be more severely damaged than either he or his friend realized. To cut operating costs, Norio outsourced the warehousing and shipping of its products to another distributor. Then when relations with that distributor deteriorated, he was left without a backup plan. Having had enough, his friend pulled the plug, and the company was liquidated. JoAnne, in a state of crisis over the uncertainty of their circumstances, told him she wanted to separate. Norio, standing in his kitchen, realized once and for all that life was not going to turn out.

Driving was what Norio knew best. It was also what he loved. Employment, however, was not a given. Yes, his class A commercial license was enough to get him lower-paying work running regional routes for local companies. But what he was after were the long hauls and higher rates offered by the big companies, and because he had been away from trucking for close to ten years, he was treated by these companies as a novice. He was told to go back to driving school and then to hire on as a trainee.

One month of driving school out of the way, he secured a position as a trainee with a firm out of Olathe, Kansas. Soon he was instated as a driver, and thirteen months later he moved to another employer out of Charlotte, North Carolina. This was in February 2004. Only now did he settle into this new way of life. The cab of his eighteen-wheeler became home, and the bunk behind the seat, his bed. He was driving from coast to coast and to points in between, much of the driving done at night, and he logged on average 12,000 miles per month, 144,000 miles per year. Life was not going to turn out, but every day was going to be a new adventure. His windshield became his window on the world.

3

THE GREAT LIFE

MICHIO KUSHI, NORIO'S FATHER, CAME from Japan to
the United States in 1949 to pursue international law at
Columbia University. His mission in life, he had already
decided, was to contribute to the establishment of world
peace.

Michio belonged to one of the first post-war
graduating classes of Tokyo University, Japan's most
prestigious institution of higher learning. One day
while in graduate school at that same institution, he saw
a notice about a meeting of the Japan chapter of the
World Federalists Movement and decided to attend.
The meeting convened just across the Tama River
from Tokyo in Kanagawa Prefecture in the humble

residence of the Movement's Japan Representative, one Sakurazawa Yukikazu, better known in the West as George Ohsawa.

Stricken by tuberculosis in his late teens, Ohsawa discovered the curative dietary regimen of a turn-of-the-century military doctor, Ishizuka Sagen, who advocated the consumption of unpolished brown rice over that of white rice, the staple of the Japanese diet. Adopting Ishizuka's recommendations, Ohsawa overcame his disease. Then, after extensive readings in Oriental philosophy and medicine, as well as Western philosophy and science, he expanded upon Ishizuka's conclusions and authored his own comprehensive approach to questions of human health and happiness. This practical philosophy he called macrobiotics, meaning "the great life."

The first step toward living fully and freely, Ohsawa declared, was to take personal responsibility for one's physical health and wellbeing. And that could be achieved by exercising discretion as to what one ate. The infallible compass by which one was to be guided in making life choices, including choices in diet, was what he called the Unique Principal, the principal of change as manifested through the workings of the antagonistic and complementary forces known in oriental cosmology as yin and yang.

Ohsawa had a voracious intellect. He read at lightning speed and wrote prolifically. He was also a fervent internationalist. During his twenties, while engaged in import-export trade, he traveled repeatedly to Europe and learned French. Then, in 1929, at thirty-six, he settled in Paris for six years. He wrote and published several books in French on oriental medicine and Japanese culture and established a small but loyal European following that would eventually grandfather the post-war European macrobiotic movement. And when he realized his birth name was too much of a mouthful for the European palate, he began calling himself Georges Ohsawa (Georges became George when his books were translated into English).

During the war years, Ohsawa actively opposed Japan's decision to go to war, publishing books and leaflets critical of governmental policy and even participating in plots to derail the war effort. He was imprisoned and tortured and was awaiting execution when the war came to an end.

Post war, he found a new following among disaffected youth. The war had devastated Japan spiritually as well as materially, and this new breed, predominantly in their late teens and early twenties, was searching for meaning and direction. He resumed advocacy of macrobiotics with renewed zeal under the auspices of what he called the Nihon C.I., the initials standing for Centre Ignoramus, signifying the acknowledgement of human ignorance as the necessary first step on the path to discovery.

And the relationship between macrobiotics and World Federalism? What surer path to agreement between nations and among peoples than to bring to their attention the importance of eating in harmony with the ebb and flow of the universal order! The World Federalists were proponents of world government. The movement had pre-war roots but had surged in strength immediately following the war, and Ohsawa had been quick to secure the role of Japan Representative when the first international alliance of World Federalists was founded in the United States in 1947. His Japan membership was composed almost exclusively of his live-in students, the members of the Nihon C.I.

When Michio met him, Ohsawa was in his late fifties. Michio, whose association with the Nihon C.I. was brief and as an outsider, was drawn to him less for his dietary recommendations than for his breadth of vision, depth of intellect, and infective joie de vivre. And when a leading proponent of the World Federalists movement, journalist and peace activist Norman Cousins, visited Tokyo, Ohsawa arranged for Michio to meet him. Over lunch at the Imperial Hotel, Cousins wrote Michio a letter he was to show to the American authorities. Japan was still under occupation, and overseas travel by its citizens was severely restricted; but with this letter, naming Cousins as his sponsor, Michio was able to secure a much-coveted travel visa to the United States. Soon after, he was aboard a steamship bound for San Francisco.

The real import of George Ohsawa's teachings, Michio would later say, did not reveal itself to him until after he had taken up residence in New York. He was stunned by the diversity of people he encountered. People of not only different ethnicities and skin colors but of all different shapes and proportions. Such extreme disparities among the same human family had been unimaginable to him prior to his stepping outside homogeneous Japan. Given these differences, was there any hope of ever realizing world peace?

Deeply troubled by the all-too-evident disconnect between the ideals of justice being taught at Columbia and the realities of global discord, he left school. He entered something of a dark night of the soul, standing in torment for hours at a time on Fifth Avenue and in Times Square, watching people walk by. Until one day, he says, it hit him. In a world going increasingly mad, the only hope of peace was to help people regain their sanity. And the only way to do that was to give them back their internal compasses, their intuitive bearings on truth, from which they could exercise more enlightened judgment. This was what Ohsawa had meant when he said the dialectical principle of change and its application to diet was essential to world peace. Social change, to be sustainable, had to begin at the biological level; only when people began to take responsibility for their lives, including their health, could happiness and harmony be restored to families, societies, and nations.

Easier said than done, however. In these early years, most of Michio's time was devoted to just making a living. But if his attempts to start a macrobiotic movement in New York failed to attract much attention locally, they did attract one Tomoko Yokoyama, known as Aveline within the Nihon C.I. (Just as he had chosen to call himself George, Ohsawa bestowed Western nicknames on many of his students: Herman and Cornelia Aihara, Alcan Yamaguchi, and Roland Sato would also join Michio in New York. Michio remained Michio only because he had never formally been part of the Nihon C.I.)

Aveline knew Michio only through letters read aloud by Ohsawa at his evening lectures. But following her feelings, just as she later counseled Norio to do, she appeared on his doorstep in 1951. They were married three years later in 1954.

Not until George Ohsawa visited America for the first time, from late 1959 to early 1960, did the New York macrobiotics initiative begin to gain traction. Ohsawa returned that summer to conduct a two-month-long summer camp on Long Island, and a food store and a restaurant were opened in Manhattan.

Then, in 1961, in response to Ohsawa's premonition that the world was on the brink of nuclear disaster and that New York was soon to become ground zero, some thirty-four macrobiotic practitioners, including twelve children, packed into a caravan of automobiles and left for Chico, California. Herman and Cornelia Aihara were among them; Michio, Aveline, and Roland Sato stayed behind. The Cuban Missile Crisis occurred the following year.

The movement was delivered an all-but-fatal blow when Ohsawa died suddenly in 1966 at the age of seventy-three. Only after the Kushis moved to Cambridge and then Brookline did their efforts to generate interest in Ohsawa's teachings really take hold. In choosing Cambridge, Michio's strategy had been to attract bright young minds from the halls of Harvard and MIT; when he pulled in his net, however, what he came up with were flower children. A whole contingent of his earliest students traveled to Boston directly from the Haight-Ashbury District of San Francisco.

This was the sixties, and that decade's hallmark combination of hedonism and social self-righteousness was in full swing. Even the academic institutions of Boston and Cambridge were being ravaged by post-modern cultural pluralism, the notion that anything goes gaining ever more legitimacy. National morals and pride were being compromised by a meaningless war in a far-off place called Vietnam, and youth was turning on, tuning in, dropping out, and protesting anything and everything that so much as hinted of authority. But in parallel with, and to some extent even in reaction to, the psychedelic revolution and the opening of the doors of perception, there was a surge of interest in Eastern religions and mysticism, including disciplines like yoga and meditation.

Macrobiotics was an odd fit. In many ways, the values it espoused were eminently conservative. It protested the use of psychedelics as a crime against the human body and the order of the universe. It made light of religious and mystical practices unless they were coupled with a puritanical dietary regime. And it upheld many of the same traditional social values, such as the sanctity of family and the domestic role of women, that the youth movement was doing its best to tear down. But this was not necessarily the way macrobiotics was perceived by the people who came to it. What caught the attention of many was its novelty and oriental underpinnings; after all, its chief proponents were all Japanese! Nor was the value of this appeal lost on the movement's leaders. George Ohsawa published his first book in English under the title *Zen Macrobiotics*, and the specific dietary recommendations he espoused were unapologetically tied to the foodstuffs and cultural practices of his country of origin.

The Kushis established study houses, live-in houses of learning modeled after Ohsawa's Nihon C.I., and these houses, beholden to Ohsawa's teachings, promoted a culture that was cultishly pseudo-Japanese. Almost as a rite of passage, men discarded their beads and sandals and shaved and cut their hair back to 1950s lengths, while women donned ankle-length dresses and pinned their hair up in buns. The houses themselves, predominantly of Victorian vintage with high ceilings and turreted gables, were sparsely furnished. Shoes were left at the door, and occupants sat on floor cushions and slept on futons.

At mealtimes, residents convened in the houses' communal dining rooms and took seats—on floor cushions, of course—around long low tables as plates of macrobiotic fare prepared by the designated cooks, almost always women, appeared from the kitchens. Miso soup was served in traditional red-black lacquer bowls and brown rice in rice bowls. Everyone ate with chopsticks. As one of the dictums of macrobiotics was to chew solid food until you could drink it, conversation was all but replaced by the clunking of molars.

The food itself was predominantly brown: brown rice, beans, miso, soy sauce. Even the tea, made from winter harvestings of tea twigs that had been roasted once by the manufacturer and then again in the kitchen, was brown. What little color there was came from sparse portions of well-cooked seasonal vegetables.

At the height of the macrobiotic community's growth in and around Boston in the 1970s, there were some seven official study houses in Brookline, Cambridge, and even as far away as Wakefield, twenty miles out, off Route 128, as well as numerous other shared houses and apartments operated by study-house graduates. The total macrobiotic population in and around the city swelled into the thousands. And to support this subculture and its lifestyle, the Kushis founded businesses: a food store, a food packaging and distribution company, two restaurants, a book store, and two publishers of periodicals. Many of the study houses' residents found employment in these businesses, while many others held "normal" jobs in and around the city.

Twice a week, on Tuesday and Thursday evenings, Michio would lecture in downtown Boston at the

Arlington Street Church on the corner of Arlington and Boylston Streets. Members of the community would congregate to hear his latest observations regarding human physiology and physiognomy, on how the distribution of the planets in the solar system described a geometric spiral, on humanity's ancient history as revealed through arcane Japanese texts, on the secret life of bees, and more—all delivered in his strongly accented English but nevertheless made brilliantly clear through his expositions of the macrobiotic dialectic of yin and yang. Invariably, his lectures would point to the importance of eating well and of practicing macrobiotics to achieve one's dream, so that, when everyone piled into their automobiles to return home, they did so with renewed conviction and enthusiasm.

But the real clincher to Michio's lectures was that macrobiotics worked! Whatever it was in the beginning that attracted people to the Kushis' study houses, in the end it didn't matter. Once they began cleaning up their eating habits, their outlook on life changed. They stood taller. They lost weight and became more active. Their complexions became clear and radiant. Just as Ohsawa and Kushi had promised, they *did* become healthier; they *did* become happier; and they *did* become more productive.

This was the cultural milieu into which Norio was born. He remembers George Ohsawa as the grandfather-like figure with an enormous heart who visited from time to time. And he grew up in large houses shared with kooky boarders: people with strange ideas, strange habits, and extreme hang-ups regarding food (I know because I was one of them).

Many of these same people, however, also turned out to be capable entrepreneurs. They built successful businesses in the food and publishing industries and pioneered the then radical and now mainstream movement toward more natural and organic foods. Leading that movement, up until its demise in 1981, was the Kushis' natural food company, Erewhon.

Macrobiotics, as it was practiced in Boston in the 1960s and 1970s, ultimately turned out to be far too narrow a sieve to contain the energy and enthusiasm of its youthful practitioners. Even the dietary recommendations of Ohsawa and Kushi proved too rigorous and even off-center for most. But the vision of affecting social change through the promotion of a healthy lifestyle coupled with a resilient faith in the order of the universe carried itself forward in ways that may have exceeded even those teachers' wildest expectations.

By the time Norio began driving big rigs on the open road, people he had known since childhood, people once or still associated with macrobiotics and the natural foods industry, had fanned out across the country, giving him a network of friends stretching literally from coast to coast. His highway miles have consistently been punctuated by visits with these friends, and he has served, especially prior to the birth of social media, as a courier of news and information.

Macrobiotics is integral to Norio's story and his perspective on life. It is in his blood and bones. It is both family and community, and it has defined his preferences in food, his closest circle of friends, and his most fundamental beliefs about human dignity and the natural order.

That said, he keeps a healthy distance from its darker underside. He gives wide berth to the dogmas and fixations regarding food and diet perpetuated among many macrobiotic practitioners, and he is uninterested in macrobiotic-inspired idealism.

One day, when in his twenties, Norio sat together with his father sipping coffee at a Dunkin' Donuts in Brookline that Michio frequented. Michio's book *One Peaceful World* had just been published, and Norio, who didn't usually read his father's books, had taken time to read it. What had he thought? "Peace is not something that can be brought about," he said. "It doesn't occur inside of time."

Michio looked surprised and asked him to explain. Norio paused to consider the question.

"I don't know," he answered.

Michio understood him to be saying he couldn't explain because he wasn't clear what he meant. But Norio's answer was based on a feeling, not an idea; it was the feeling that he couldn't adequately explain. To him, "I don't know" was the only reasonable answer.

Years later, he would learn to speak about this incident more intelligibly. He didn't know how peace came about because such was unknowable. The world has never seen peace, so how could the manner of its conception be known? Moreover, a movement—any movement—is about external change, whereas peace is a state of being. To attempt to bring about peace through change is a bit like attempting to bring about water through stirring. World peace, if or when it comes, will come not through action or human doing but as an emergent quality of collective human maturity.

Norio has also always been amused and sometimes embarrassed by the ways in which some macrobiotic practitioners placed his father and mother on pedestals. Michio, especially, was gifted with a powerful charisma, a gift he used skillfully to inspire people all over the world to lead more responsible and productive lives. Some of these people, however, mistook the man for his message and adopted him as a role model. They took to dressing like him and parroting his explanations— even, in some instances, adopting his accented, non-native English expressions.

Growing up in this environment, Norio quickly learned that the Kushi name was both an asset and a liability. The name gave him instant recognition within the macrobiotic community and beyond, and it opened doors. But it also placed him ever in his father's long shadow. Much of his life has been about escaping that shadow and building a life of his own. Under Michio and Aveline, he received the most liberal of upbringings; they were not ones to impose their aspirations on their children. That said, given the significance of macrobiotics to their lives and livelihoods, they could not help but to project an unspoken expectation that Norio and his siblings would, each in his or her own way, continue the work they had begun.

The common-sense aspects of macrobiotics—the obvious relevance of diet to health and wellbeing and the thereby implicit importance of natural, whole, and organic foods, for example—as well as George Ohsawa's vision of a "great life" are precepts to which

Norio wholeheartedly subscribes. Nevertheless, he has never aspired to teach or to extol the benefits of the macrobiotic lifestyle. He has never considered standing, as did his father, in front of audiences to explain the natural world in terms of the workings of yin and yang.

Norio's realization that life was not going to turn out and the renunciation of living for a future can also be characterized as the acceptance of responsibility in much the way that George Ohsawa had indicated necessary if one were to aspire to freedom. A life that is not going to turn out is a life that can only be lived. A life with no future is also a life with no past. The day he decides to go back to driving a truck, he also steps out of his father's shadow.

4

A Personal Project

Command of a big rig affords Norio both freedoms and restraints. On the one hand, the ever-changing landscapes and the long hours alone in his cab are conducive to contemplation, and he makes of driving what others might call a meditative practice. On the other, he is beholden to the demands of his profession. He has deadlines to meet and orders to fulfill, and he is navigating a machine of enormous mass over heavily traveled highways. His employer, their clients, and other drivers on the road count on him to not allow his attention to stray far from the highway lines ahead.

As he settles into his new routine in February 2004, Norio is content. Long hours behind the wheel suit him, and he is immune to monotony; he hasn't known boredom since he left school. Furthermore, within the radically new space he now occupies, that of not living for a future, time takes on a different feel. Every mile is new, no matter how many times he has driven it before, and no matter how many miles he logs, he can never put distance between himself and the present. The landscape might be ever-changing, but his experience of being alive and in the driver's seat has a quality of timeless continuity.

Not that he has walked away from his old habits. He is still Norio. He still has his past, his likes and dislikes, his shortcomings and challenges. And he still has his problems. Especially money problems. There is never enough money. He is paid by the mile, and every mile driven seems to fall just short of bills coming due back home.

Then there are his relationships. He and JoAnne, though separated, talk regularly by phone. They talk about the kids and about finances. But why is it, even though their interests are aligned, they talk past rather than to each other? Why do they talk around their problems rather than toward solutions?

His children are growing up quickly, each encountering new choices and challenges. How can he be the father he needs to be to all six of them while living out of a truck?

These and other concerns play over and over in his mind as he drives. Not that dwelling on them is ever going to produce solutions; thinking about his problems, he understands, is futile. But that doesn't stop the thoughts from coming.

"Wait, though," it occurs to him. Is he alone in having to deal with problems? Of course not. Problems aren't unique to him; everyone has problems. Everyone who has ever lived has had them.

Why is it people all have problems? Why is it that having problems seems to be inherent to humanness? And if problems are universal, then what is he to make of the problem of having problems? Is it really a problem that there are problems? Or is it just part of the way life is and is supposed to be?

These questions put his problems in a new light. He is seeing them not just as the stuff of his personal conundrum but also as that of the collective experience. Evidently, he is far less special than he thought; he is simply human. He might just as well consider himself a representative sample picked randomly from among his species.

And in this, he sees a project worth pursuing. The project is to observe what it is to be human. No lofty aspirations involved here; no amateur attempt at philosophy. His project is but a personal hobby, and it is not about conjecture but about fact finding. He, Norio, is human; based on that incontrovertible given, what can he observe about the human condition?

As a child, he had been fascinated by hand-held puzzles, like the ones made from interlocking rings or pieces of wood. He had spent hours figuring out how to take those puzzles apart and then to put them back together. Now he approaches the question "What is it to be human?" as such a puzzle, as a source of amusement, and with a similarly childlike fascination. His excitement is such that he wants to tell someone about it, so he calls his friend Ben.

"I'm studying the human condition in the way an entomologist studies a butterfly," he announces.

Ben has nothing to say.

He is studying humanness, Norio goes on to explain, by using himself as a specimen. He is studying this human specimen with an eye for detail but with total suspension of judgment. What entomologist, after all, passes judgment on a butterfly? To an entomologist, there are no good butterflies or bad butterflies, only butterflies worthy of study. The same applies to Norio's study. In it, there will be neither good human habits nor bad human habits, just habits. He is after data, not the assignment of value to that data.

It is fun. It gives him something more to do as he drives. When one of those pesky four-wheelers—trucker lingo for automobiles—cuts him off in traffic, he observes his reactions. When he pulls into a truck stop, he watches how he interacts with fellow members of his species. He makes mental notes but draws no conclusions. He has no purpose or goal, nor does he anticipate that the project will lead to anything useful.

The act of making his subjective experience an object of study allows him a novel perspective on the world, and he is continually surprised by what he finds. Ordinary events cease to be ordinary; each is a new clue as to what it means to be human.

He was heading east across Nevada on Interstate 80. His thoughts turned to JoAnne. More accurately, they turned to his breakup with JoAnne and how painful it had been. The memory was wrapped in intense sorrow.

What next caught his attention, however, was not the details of the memory, details he had played over in his mind far too often, but the visceral way in which the sorrow induced by the memory arose within. The feeling was something quite separate from the memory. Yes, the memory had acted as a trigger. It was almost as if the mind had said, "This memory calls for sorrow," and the body had responded. But the sorrow itself arose from somewhere other than the memory. It arose first from within his gut and then spread into the organs and tissue of his chest.

Furthermore, this feeling of sorrow was clearly not unique to this occasion. It was the enactment of a pre-existent capacity for sorrow. The sorrow was already there, dormant, just waiting to be awakened. It was just waiting to be prompted to express itself.

That the memory of his breakup should evoke such sorrow was not news. The novelty was in the observation that, whereas before he would have said he felt sorrow because of the breakup, he now saw the breakup and the experience of sorrow as associated but not causally related. The memory was the memory, the sorrow was the sorrow. Because they arose together, the mind interpreted them as one movement, but such was not the reality. Each occurred independently of the other.

The moment this became clear to him—the moment the cause-effect relationship between his memory of the breakup and his felt sorrow was severed—the memory fell away. Only the sorrow remained. But to his continuing astonishment, almost immediately, another memory, also associated with sorrow, arose to take the first memory's place.

He looked at this new memory as he had the first and soon saw that it, too, was not in and of itself the cause of the sorrow it evoked. It only suggested to some part of his mind that sorrow was an appropriate response, and the mind then took that suggestion and called upon the pre-existent reservoir of sorrow he held within. Again, as soon as he saw this, the new memory also fell away.

He had an almost limitless library of memories associated with sorrow, and he watched as they lined up and took turns at bat. Past relationships, misfortunes, the death of his mother, the death of his sister—the list went on and on. Each of these memories surfaced in turn. And each in turn, when he severed it from the bodily sensation of sorrow, fell away.

Memories arose and fell in this way for mile after mile. They toppled like dominoes, and the speed with which they fell, slow at first, accelerated over time. Tears streamed down his face. Not only did he relive each memory, he also savored it. And he savored the sorrow associated with it. His were tears of relief as well as pain.

When the last of the dominoes fell, he was crossing the Great Salt Flats, approaching Salt Lake City. The sun had gone down behind him, and he was driving into darkness. All the memories were gone. All that was left was the sorrow. And the sorrow, he knew, was not going away.

It was not going away because, unlike memory, it was not something acquired through experience. It was part of the human condition. Until now, he had treated sorrow like a personal problem. He had spent an inordinate amount of energy attempting to manage it, attempting to either control or avoid it. But the sorrow was not his to control or avoid. What he was experiencing was not Norio sorrow; it was human sorrow. His sorrow was drawn from a communal waterhole from which all humanity drank, and that waterhole had existed from long before he was born and would presumably continue to exist long after he was gone.

In the days and weeks following his insight into the nature of sorrow, several changes occurred in the way he, Norio, functioned as a human specimen. First, sorrow ceased to exercise control over him. The sorrow was still there; he could call it up with ease. But he was no longer at its mercy. He no longer identified with it. It was just sorrow, just another feature to be noted and indexed in his growing list of observations concerning the human condition.

Second, when he looked into the faces of the people he encountered, people at truck stops and at points of pickup and delivery, he saw the same sorrow. He saw it in their eyes. They were all so heavily invested, just as he had been, in managing their sorrow, in suppressing and denying it. He felt their pain as his own. And he also felt their sorrow on another level; he felt sorry for the enormous waste of human vitality being perpetrated in the name of avoiding sorrow. Attempting to suppress and deny sorrow only served to reinforce it, to make it more intransigent. Moreover, such suppression and denial were a collective enterprise; humanity, it seemed, was intent upon perpetuating the myth that avoidance of sorrow was key to happiness.

The word suggested to him by these feelings was compassion. But to say he felt compassion for his fellow man was both inadequate and misleading, since "compassion for" suggested a he and a they. The compassion he felt was more like a disintegration of the distinction between self and other. And this had implications for his personal project. He could no longer be the disinterested observer because the observer and the observed appeared to be one and the same.

In September 2004, Norio picks up a load in Rialto, California, off Interstate 10, near San Bernardino. He checks in at the guard shack, drops his empty trailer in a designated parking space, and backs his cab into the loaded trailer he is to take to Tracy, fifty miles south of Stockton, an easy drive up Interstate 5. The day is getting on, so he will do a third of the trip this evening, spending the night at a truck stop in Buttonwillow, near Bakersfield, and the remainder in the morning.

The trailer hooked, he pulls his rig onto the shipper's scales. Not all shippers are considerate enough to provide such facilities. California's fines are the highest in the country, so this opportunity is not to be missed. Satisfied to see his truck has weighed in well within legal limits, he proceeds to the guard shack for checkout.

As he is speaking with the guard through his cab window, he feels a peculiar rocking sensation. It is almost as if he is aboard a boat at sea. The sensation is disconcerting; he has never experienced anything like it before.

Papers in hand and cleared to leave, he pulls out of the lot onto the street. The rocking sensation intensifies. Something is clearly not right. He drives around the corner, parks, and calls his dispatcher.

He's not feeling well, he explains. He doesn't think it safe for him to drive. Is there someone in the area who can take over?

No, the dispatcher informs him. He has no other drivers anywhere nearby. But the company does have a yard in Fontana, just five miles away.

Five miles is doable, Norio concedes. He will drive to Fontana and drop the truck at the yard.

"Drive safely," the dispatcher cautions.

The sun has set, and twilight descends. Over the course of the mile and a half to Interstate 10, the rocking sensation becomes ever more uncomfortable and disconcerting. Nevertheless, he pulls onto the freeway. Soon after, however, the rocking from side to side becomes a full-revolution spin. Everything in his field of vision, including the dashboard and windshield of his truck, is rotating clockwise in front of his eyes.

Glancing down, he can barely make out his dashboard's display, but he musters just enough focus to decipher that he is traveling at thirty miles an hour. Traffic to his left is racing by at seventy, eighty, and above.

"This won't do," he thinks. "Better to get off the highway and take side roads to Fontana." This is a reasonable plan; he knows his way, as he drives in this area often.

Darkness has set in when he exits at Sierra Avenue. Not that he can read the exit sign; it is spinning beyond recognition. But he knows these exits by heart, and Sierra is next. Clinging to the yellow line marking the freeway's edge, he bears right onto the exit ramp.

He also knows there is a set of traffic lights at the top of the ramp. When he looks up, however, all he can see is a Christmas-like montage of colored lights, all spinning so incoherently as to make it impossible to say which are the traffic lights.

He pulls the truck over to the side of the exit ramp, stops, pulls the brake, and sits. As he sits, he is overcome with nausea. He climbs out of the cab, goes around it to the side of the road, gets down on all fours, and vomits violently into the grass. He vomits again and again. At last, his stomach settles down.

But the world is still incoherent. It is spinning so wildly he has lost all bearing on up and down, right and left. When he goes to stand, he immediately keels over. He has no balance. He tries again; the same thing happens. He crawls on hands and knees back to the cab and pulls himself up into the driver's seat. Then he lays his head on the wheel.

"Eventually, this will pass," he thinks to himself. All he can do is wait.

Many minutes have passed when he becomes aware that his cab is being illuminated by flashing blue lights. The lights, he sees when he lifts his head, are coming from a motorcycle. A police officer is standing outside his door.

The police officer mounts the step of his cab and puts his head in through the open window. "Are you OK?" he asks.

"No, I'm not, Officer," Norio replies. He is feeling sick. It isn't safe for him to drive.

"I have no idea what is happening," he continues.

As they talk, a firetruck pulls up in front. In his distracted state, Norio wonders if there is a fire somewhere. But in short order, two firemen are standing beside the police officer and asking, "Can we check you out?"

"I'm not able to stand," he tells them.

"No problem. We'll hold you up." One fireman on each arm, they lift him from the cab and practically carry him to the back of their truck. There, they hook him up to equipment they carry on board and take his vital signs.

"I'm not getting anything," says the man measuring his blood pressure. "Let's try the other arm."

The thought runs through Norio's mind that perhaps he has been in a horrific accident. Perhaps he is dead. But the thought is fleeting. His other arm shows his blood pressure to be normal; evidently, he is still alive.

Now the police officer is asking, "Can someone move the truck?" Norio instructs him to retrieve his cellphone from the cab and hits the redial button, connecting it again with the dispatcher. He hands the phone to the police officer. His world still spinning out of control, he loses track of the conversation but learns from the officer after he finishes the call that his dispatcher has agreed to allow the truck to be towed and impounded on a police lot until another driver can be sent to claim it.

Momentarily, an ambulance also arrives. "I think you need to go to the hospital," the policeman says as he hands him back his phone.

Until now, Norio has been watching these events unfold in a dreamlike state of detachment. But his reaction to the officer's words is visceral. Every fiber of his being resists. He has never been a patient in a hospital, and his macrobiotic upbringing has instilled in him a deep-seated suspicion of the medical establishment and its practices. He, Norio, being taken by ambulance to a hospital? No way.

This dialogue, however, is all internal; he says nothing to the police officer.

Then the entomologist in him kicks in. The human specimen he is now observing has no idea what is going on with it physically. For all it knows, its condition may be permanent. It is unable to drive, unable to walk, unable to function. That it does not want to go to the hospital has no bearing on reality or the gravity of its situation. It is at the mercy of these people who have so graciously appeared out of nowhere to rescue it. Of course he will go to the hospital. He has no choice.

The moment of concession is followed by one of relief. In saying "Yes" to the officer, he surrenders to the unknown. He gives up all claim to personal volition. How curious the notion that life should be self-determined?

Will he ever return to normal? Will he be able to continue his occupation and to support his family? Will he ever be able to function again as a contributing member of society? Right now, the answers to these questions are not for him to know. His "yes" is not just a yes to the hospital; it's a yes to a life over which he exercises no control.

He is given an IV and strapped into a stretcher. Soon, they are moving. They are going, one of the EMTs tells him, to the Kaiser Permanente Hospital in Fontana. He summons just enough presence of mind to hit the speed-dial on his phone for a lady-friend named Rachel in Los Angeles, and she picks up. Could she meet him at the hospital in Fontana, he asks after explaining, in a couple of sentences, what has happened. She agrees. Then he falls asleep.

He awakens briefly when they arrive at the hospital, for he remembers being wheeled inside. Then he falls off again.

The next time he awakes, he is in a hospital room. How much time has transpired, he cannot say. But the spinning sensation has ceased, and his vision and equilibrium have been restored. A doctor is in the room, as is Rachel.

It was vertigo, the doctor explains. It was caused by an inner ear infection. Five days of antibiotics and he will be fine. (Norio fills the prescription but never takes the medication.) Discharged, he rides home with Rachel to Los Angeles.

The incident has repercussions. His company takes him off the road for a week and requires an opinion from a specialist before recertifying him. But those seven days are infused with grace. He is at peace. He is grateful to be alive.

5

THE ENDING OF TIME

THE GRACE THAT DESCENDED UPON him during his week of recuperation in Los Angeles followed him back to work. No longer under any illusion of control over life, the day-to-day business of living became effortless. His days dawned fresh and new. He felt incessantly lighthearted and joyful. Why he should feel such unencumbered happiness, he couldn't say; certainly not because he had done anything to deserve it. It was simply what showed up in the absence of ambition and the desire to succeed.

One year earlier, in October 2003, Norio saw something in a magazine about a twenty-one-year-old named

Jonathan Meier walking from Portland, Maine, to San Francisco in the name of peace. Meier's "Walk for Peace" was partially inspired by Ohio congressman Dennis Kucinich, who had recently announced his intentions to run for president. Among his many causes, Kucinich was an advocate and defender of natural agriculture, and he was also a good friend of the Kushi family. Largely through Kucinich's influence, the Smithsonian Institution established a permanent archive documenting Michio and Aveline's macrobiotic activities and their influence on American society. Photographs and artifacts from the archive were put on display at the National Museum of American History in Washington, D.C., for two months in 1999.

To walk across the country. What an interesting undertaking! "I'd like to meet this Jonathan Meier," Norio thought. "I'd like to meet him in Kansas," he thought next. Why Kansas, he had no idea; it was just what popped up.

That was it—just a passing thought. As with his premonition about John Lennon's visit, he did not dwell on it. Once the thought passed, he put it out of mind.

Some four months later, in late January 2004, he picks up a load of paper outside of Dallas, Texas, for delivery to Kansas City. The shipper has no scales on premises, but Norio is sure the load is overweight (a weigh-in at a truck stop later confirms this to be so). For a moment, he considers asking for a re-load, a demand within his rights. But then, he wants to be going. He will just circumvent the weigh stations.

There are four weigh stations between him and his destination, two in Oklahoma and two in Kansas. He puts a call out over citizens band radio to truckers southbound on Interstate 35 and learns that the Oklahoma stations and one of the Kansas stations are closed but that the Kansas station south of Wichita is open. He checks his maps and plots his route.

Traveling north on Interstate 35 toward Wichita, he misses his exit. No worry; there is one more exit before the weigh station. He takes it and doubles back.

Then, however, he misses the turn he needs to put him back on track. He makes a calculated guess, turns at an intersection, and compounds his error. One more wrong turn lands him far east of where he wants to be.

Four wrong turns. Norio is not infallible; he makes a wrong turn now and again. But four in a row is unheard of. And these on the plains of Kansas, where almost all the roads run either north-south or east-west like lines on a checkerboard. It's a first in his history of driving.

This is when it occurs to him, "There must be something else going on!" No sooner does he think the thought than he catches sight of two figures walking ahead of him along the side of the road. It is Jonathan Meier and a companion—her name is Amy, he learns—on the walk for peace.

Too late to stop, he passes, turns around, passes again, turns around again, and stops just beyond them, pulling his truck well over to the side of the road. He hops out of his cab, approaches, and introduces himself. His name is Norio Kushi, he is a friend of Dennis Kucinich, and he has heard about Jonathan's walk for peace and has stopped to meet him.

After delivering his load in Kansas City, Norio catches up with the party again that evening at a Dennis Kucinich campaign rally in Wichita. And two months later, Norio's brother Hal is one of the organizers of a Kucinich rally in Oakland, California, also attended by Jonathan who has just completed his walk. Hal introduces himself as a brother of "the truck driver who stopped to meet you in Kansas."

Several months prior to seeing the article about Jonathan Meier, Norio delivered a load from Nebraska to Pennsylvania. He calls JoAnne from Council Bluffs, Iowa, to talk about his plans to return to Asheville over the weekend.

"I'll be bringing two evergreen bushes back with me," he tells her. The announcement is out of the blue. Norio has no idea what prompts him to say this; it just comes out.

What will they do with two evergreen bushes? The implication is that JoAnne will need to plant them, and she objects.

"No, don't worry," he assures her. He will take care of the planting.

After unloading north of Pittsburgh, he calls in for his next assignment. The dispatcher sends him to a tree farm in Erie to pick up a load of trees and shrubs for delivery to multiple locations in and around Kansas City. He drives to Kansas City and makes the rounds. After his last stop, he looks in the back of the truck. Two evergreens remain. They are left over and unaccounted for on the bills of lading. He takes them into the cab with him back to Asheville and plants them in the yard.

As with the John Lennon story, these two anecdotes challenge conventional wisdom regarding the nature of time. The phenomenon of time is ordinarily understood to be the narrative of change. That narrative includes a past, living in memory; a present, living in experience; and a future, living in imagination.

The future might also be described as a probability cloud containing all the innumerable possible outcomes of a succession of events but favoring some outcomes over others. When that future becomes the present, the cloud collapses, and one of the possibilities is singled out and made fact.

But is that so? Or if it is, then how was Norio to account for his propensity for imagining futures that came to be? How is it that he imagined John Lennon in his living room or Jonathan Meier in Kansas? Indeed, ever since his mother told him to trust his feelings, Norio has had numerous such experiences, always with the same sense of certainty.

Is it because he had a special ability? That ability, should it exist, would necessarily be supernatural, for it would defy the fundamentally inviolable law that time moves in one direction only, away from certainty and toward uncertainty.

Or to adopt a much-espoused New Age interpretation, was Norio creating his future by visualizing it? Was the real world malleable to human will and the workings of mind?

Neither of these interpretations was satisfactory. He didn't consider himself specially endowed, and he didn't have any sense that he was causing these random future events to occur by imagining them. It was a mystery. He could say no more.

Upon picking up a new load, Norio, out of habit, would perform a simple ritual. Once his truck was loaded and his paperwork in order, he would sit quietly in his cab and imagine his arrival at his destination. It took no more than a moment.

He attached no special importance to this ritual; he wasn't superstitious. He only found it calming and reassuring. It put him in a state of readiness and focused his attention on the drive ahead.

On this morning in the fall of 2004, he had just received a load outside of Philadelphia for delivery to California. He was all set to go. He sat, took a breath, and imagined his arrival at the yard in California.

Instead of just the image of his arrival, however, he was given an image of the entire journey as a single event, one where beginning and end occurred simultaneously.

It was another instance of his "felt" intuition speaking. He recognized it immediately for its signature clarity. This was neither an idea nor a concept. He was being shown, first hand, another perspective on time. From that perspective, the notion of linear time was a fiction, a creation of the mind.

One of the challenges of describing this insight, he has since come to realize, is that the structure of language, beholden as it is to subjects and predicates, calls forth the very concepts of linear progression and of cause and effect that he is seeking to question. But all one can do is try.

The metaphor that came to mind was that of an arrow being released from a bow. For practical purposes, the arrow's flight is determined upon its release, and we experience the flight of the arrow and its arrival at its target as a single event. The mind, unless it is engaged in the study of calculus, does not dwell on the succession of positions the arrow occupies in between.

In the same way, whereas until now, Norio had always conceived of his journey from start to destination to be a product of a succession of actions—of stops and starts, of turns, of detours and choices, of traffic and weather, and so on—was it not just as valid, if not more so, to conceive of the entire affair as a single event? Beginning and end were relative concepts; neither had meaning without the other. The journey was only "a journey" because it had both beginning and end.

Was not the concept of a journey as miles traveled over time elapsed, as the aggregate of a long series of momentary decisions and actions, no more than a mental deconstruction established after the fact? True, he was alive and present at every moment along the way. But was there anything to require of those moments that they construct a greater whole? Could not each be looked at as a mini-journey with a beginning and end of its own?

For two years now, Norio had been living in the absence of a future. He had given up on living life as though it was a means to an end. He had not given up, however, on the narrative that time was linear. He had not even been aware of that narrative. He was still living life as a story, as a sequence of events.

But now, just as he had been done with living for a future ever since seeing that life was not going to turn out, he was also done with life's narrative. The story, he saw, also had a beginning and an end, and it had just ended. It was over. Done.

The highway, to Norio, is a metaphor for life. Life too is a journey with a beginning and an end.

But what if all that was also just a story? What was he to make of birth and death? Was this entity he called Norio something born in time? Was it destined to disappear, to be no more? These questions were neither frightening nor daunting, just mysterious. In the context of his personal project, they were also intriguing. They were fun.

After all, he was a truck driver, not a philosopher. He wasn't after universal truth. All he could say was, for this human specimen, the time narrative was over.

The time narrative out of the equation, however, the John Lennon incident, the Jonathan Meier incident, and so many other similar incidents became plausible in a quasi-logical sort of a way. Norio was neither seeing the future nor creating it. He was simply seeing the present.

→ *future is in the Present.*
time is a fn of mind

The ending of the time narrative had several practical ramifications. These soon became apparent during his drive to California. First, his approach to traffic and the way he drove in it changed. Whereas before, he would have characterized traffic as a hindrance—he might have said to himself, "This traffic is slowing me down. It's delaying me"—he now saw it as an integral part of the one movement that was the journey. The highway took on the characteristics of a river. He was just a part of the flow, and being part of the flow required no effort. There was never, ever, anything in the way.

Instead of seeing this river as made up of vehicles, he began to see it as a spatial fabric made up of expanding and contracting intervals between vehicles. Moreover, his ability to see the flow of traffic in this way also allowed him some influence over it. "Beating the traffic" was no longer a goal; he was only playing in the river. But by playing with the space between his truck and the other vehicles, he was able, within limits, to improve the river's flow. He could introduce more uniformity of speed into the lane in which he was traveling. He could keep right or move left to pass as best served the river's purpose. Adjustments to the space ahead of him could alleviate the bunching of traffic into knots. All of which was highly entertaining; it became almost a game.

It was also productive. He kept careful logs of his mileage and hours, and his driving times consistently improved.

Finally, with the cessation of the narrative, his capacity to take anything personally all but disappeared. Where a curt remark from a sales clerk might have caused him to wonder, "What did I do wrong?" it now rolled off him like water off a duck's back; the clerk was only having a bad day. And where he had been observing himself with the scrutiny of an entomologist, he now stepped back and took a more relaxed and much broader view. The feeling was that of being perched in a theatre balcony watching little Norio act out his drama on the stage below.

6

THE SPACE BETWEEN THOUGHTS

THERE'S THAT 1970s SONG BY Albert Hammond that goes, "It never rains in southern California / But girl, don't they warn ya / It pours." Such was the case now. Torrential rains had fallen for days and were bringing down hillsides and causing flash floods from Santa Barbara to San Diego.

The date was February 6, 2005. Norio had delivered one load and was sent to pick up another, only to be told, after having been kept waiting, that the load was gone. His dispatcher had made a mistake; another driver had already taken it.

These things happen. Even though he got soaked every time he stepped out of his cab, Norio was unperturbed. Calls went back and forth, and the dispatcher sorted things out. Norio was given a new assignment. He was to pick up in Rialto from the same shipping yard in which the vertigo incident had begun almost five months earlier—his first time back there since.

At the guard shack, he was told the load would not be ready until the following morning. Again, no problem. Norio had no dog in this fight. He accepted the news and prepared to stay the night.

Although he had yet to consciously acknowledge it, he had become all but incapable of harboring discontent. Such had been the case ever since surrendering himself up to the paramedics that evening on the Sierra Avenue exit off Interstate 10. His life had become less consumed by doing, more consumed by being.

That evening, as he lay on his bunk in the back of his cab, thinking about the events of the day, he was struck by the inevitability with which any quality invoked its opposite. Just as left could not exist without right or up could not exist without down, today was a "rainy day" only because most days were sunny, while conversely the "sunny days" only existed because of the occasional rainy ones. He only got wet when he stepped outside his truck because he was dry to begin with; the very nature of dryness was dependent upon such soakings. There was something comical about it all, the way people attached such value to one quality over its opposite, even though the one could not exist without the other. Not that he was any exception; given the choice, he preferred to stay dry over getting wet. But nevertheless, it was funny.

The entire pageant of human existence was infused with this same absurd attachment to ideas. So much energy was spent in defense of beliefs when what was being defended was defined by what was being defended against. How obvious, for example, that a belief in God and a belief in no God were interdependent, that the one required the other if it was to have any meaning. And yet, people argued that one of these beliefs was right and the other wrong. They even fought wars in the name of such beliefs. How comical! He chuckled himself to sleep.

He also fell asleep with a knowing that the morning would dawn bright and clear.

It did.

He awakens on February 7 to find a message light blinking on his phone. This is his company's internal messaging system, and they want him to call. When he does, he is told he is being reassigned to pick up a load in Perris, thirty miles south on Interstate 215. The load is time sensitive; it needs to be delivered to Visalia, in the San Joaquin Valley, by seven that evening. Even allowing for L.A. traffic, this is eminently doable. The drive is only two hundred and fifty miles.

From his first seconds awake, he is aware that, overnight, something has changed. The change becomes even more palpable while he is on the phone with the dispatcher. Since beginning his personal project one year ago, that of inquiring into what it is to be human, Norio has become ever more objective in his observations and has watched with ever more detachment as the events of his life unfold. He has even applied that same objectivity to his inquiry into feelings, as he did with the relationship between memory and sorrow. Now, however, that detachment has been extended to include his thoughts. He is watching his thoughts as they occur, much as if they are being run across a digital screen placed in front of him.

More importantly, what shows up is not just the thoughts—not just their content—but the way in which they occur. They occur in patterns. This is not something he has ever noticed before. Thoughts occur as pulses or waves, originating from somewhere on the fringes of awareness, rolling in and inundating his mental space, and then receding back out to the fringes. Whatever is sending the waves forth must be like a great ocean, for the waves keep coming. But it is outside the realm of his conscious awareness. The entire process is most peculiar, most spectacular, and he watches with wonder.

The dispatcher on the line is not his usual one. Norio usually works with his fleet manager in Charlotte, North Carolina, but because the load he has just been assigned falls under the supervision of the company's southwestern district operations, he is put in touch with a dispatcher in Phoenix, Arizona. He and Norio have no history, and Norio, who accepts the Visalia job with his usual calm, evidently comes across over the phone as indifferent. The dispatcher is irritated. Does Norio understand the urgency of this assignment? Does he understand that, should the load not be delivered by seven, the company will suffer repercussions?

Yes, he understands, Norio assures him. If the dispatcher has any doubts regarding his competence and reliability, he is free to call headquarters and ask for his records. He gives the dispatcher his fleet manager as a reference, and he gives his word that the delivery will be made on time. The dispatcher is satisfied. They hang up, and Norio washes, shaves, and brews a cup of tea before setting out.

He has witnessed the entire exchange with the dispatcher, as he subsequently does those with the people at the pickup location warehouse, with detached fascination. These events are unfolding not just in physical time-space but in a human world-space made up of thoughts and communications. As he listens to what is being said, he also watches the extraordinary patterns etched on the screen in front of him by his thoughts as they ebb and flow. The strangeness of it! The self that is thinking and the self that is watching the thoughts are not the same; they are distinct.

Furthermore, in no way does that separateness interfere with or impede his ability to function. To the contrary, it enhances it. He immediately apprehends the intent of others' communications, and he translates his thoughts into words and sentences with sufficient clarity to leave no room for misunderstandings. As he enters the highway, he is fully awake to the reality of the road in front of him, even as he continues to be present to his thoughts.

The sun is bright; the sky is azure blue; he is filled with gratitude for the simple joy of being alive. On all accounts, it is a beautiful day.

He is now on a stretch of road truckers call the Grapevine. It's the section of Interstate 5 that connects the San Fernando Valley with the San Joaquin by way of Tejon Pass. He continues to watch his thoughts—both the idle ones, the sundry thoughts of what happened yesterday and of recent conversations with JoAnne and the children, and the consequential ones, such as remembering to monitor his diesel gauge and knowing when to shift gears—as they play across his mental screen.

That is when he first notices something new. As his thoughts roll in and then recede, one after another, he notices that in between the dissolution of one thought and the shaping of the next there is a space. There is an interval. It is extremely brief—so brief as to have escaped him up until now. But it's there. It catches his attention as would a shiny object. He watches the next thought recede. Sure enough, just before a new one forms, there is that space. How peculiar. What might it be?

He is driving through spectacular scenery, and he takes it in, along with the sunlight and the sky, with a sense of grace and wonder. But his attention is not on his surroundings; it is on the spectacle of his thoughts. And now, out of his innocent inquiry into the nature of thought, has come this discovery of silence.

But then, given his recognition the evening before of the inevitable complementarity of opposites, of course there is silence; thoughts could not show up otherwise. To be heard, thought requires a backdrop of silence. Now he is really intrigued. The moments of silence between thoughts command his full attention.

Then, yet another unusual development. Engrossed by the mystery of these fleeting moments of silence, he notices the moments' duration beginning to expand. They expand from a fraction of a second to a full second. Then one second becomes two, two seconds becomes five, five seconds becomes ten, and then, fifteen.

During those intervals, all thought is gone; his mind is completely quiet. He is, nevertheless, fully aware of his circumstances and surroundings. He has full control over his truck, he knows exactly where he is and where he is going, and he is acutely tuned to the presence and movements of other vehicles on the road. This is to his surprise. He has always assumed that the train of his thoughts is somehow critical to his ability to function; in fact, however, those thoughts are at best neutral, occurring as a commentary on his actions, and at worst an unnecessary hindrance.

Moreover, his actions cease to be "his"; that is, they cease to be willfully derived. They become, instead, natural consequences of the circumstances that dictate them, with the Norio person behind the wheel

Thought is temporary and fleeting and [perhaps?]... silence is [timeless?] and permanent

functioning as their agent, not their author. The Norio person's focus of attention has shifted away from the act of driving toward the spacious mental void in which driving and all other actions occur.

The primary attribute of that mental void is its utter silence, and his awareness is drawn to the silence like a moth to a flame. He exerts no effort. He need not call forth concentration nor seek to control or suppress his thinking. His attention simply follows the path of least resistance, and silence is where that path leads.

The thoughts, it is now obvious, are originating out of silence and returning to it. Thought and silence are antipodes of one movement. That said, those antipodes are not of equal stature, for where the thoughts are constantly coming and going, the silence always remains. It is ever present, either as background or as foreground. Thought is temporal and transitory; silence is timeless and permanent.

The duration of the intervals is now in the order of minutes. Silence has overtaken thought; thought has become the exception, and silence, the rule. The quietude is both empty and full. It is formless. It has no content. But at the same time, it is suffused with a presence defying all description. Call it grace. Call it equanimity. Call it unconditional love. These names and more apply, but none are remotely adequate.

Furthermore, although he has no conscious memory
of a precedent for this most unusual state of being, it
is nevertheless intimately familiar. Intuition tells him it
has always been present and that he has always known
it to be present. He senses he is home.

He stops at a truck stop. As he sits at a counter
sipping a cup of tea, he looks around. He looks at the
young people behind the counter and in the kitchen.
He looks at the other drivers perched at the counter
devouring their hamburgers and fries. He isn't special.
What is home for him is home for them too. What is
so for him is so for them too. This ground of being is
indiscriminant; it does not choose based on intelligence,
education, or ability. All of them occupy this same state
of equanimity. It's shared equally by all. The humor of
it! Each, he included, is just one more expression of a
shared humanity sitting in a truck stop somewhere in
paradise.

By the time he reaches Visalia, thought has all but ceased.
The necessary thoughts, those that guide him into the
warehouse dock and make it possible to communicate
with the workers there, come right on cue. But all the
other thoughts he is accustomed to entertaining, the
idle and speculative ones, have disappeared, much as
if the plug that feeds energy to the machine that is his

mind has been pulled from its socket. The calculating, assessing, and fantasizing mind is at rest.

Norio remains in this state of no thought for about two weeks. He does so through no conscious will or effort, for quite the opposite, he is incapable of escaping from it. Not that he has any desire to do so. He is in continuous bliss. He is also awake and aware, noticing things, places, and people such as he never has before. And in the evening, when he lays his body down and allows his senses to go to sleep, that awareness slips out of its earthly confines. It is alert even as the body sleeps, and it journeys to parts he has no words to identify or describe. Even so, it never tires. He awakes in the morning fully rested.

During these two weeks, he has almost no contact with family or friends. It isn't that he avoids such contact; it's just that it doesn't seem necessary. After all, he isn't thinking, so he doesn't have much to say. He feels no urgency to tell anyone anything about what is going on with him, especially as he cannot explain it. Nor can he even begin to describe what it is like to be in a space of no thought, as just the attempt would call on the realm of thought. As for the equanimity and love, there are some things best left unsaid because words can only belittle them.

Norio has never had any interest in religion or spiritual teachings, and consequently, he has no ready-made lexicon of spiritual terms to call upon, no framework of spiritual knowledge to apply. Were he familiar with Vedanta, for example, he might call what is happening Samadhi. Were he familiar with Buddhism, he might call it satori or enlightenment. As it is, none of these words mean anything to him, so they don't come to mind. That there might be long traditions and vast literatures describing, from a multitude of cultural perspectives, the sort of state he is witnessing is completely outside his sphere of knowledge.

He is simply resting in reality. The Norio person in his truck is but a vehicle for one perspective on the world. That world is perfect and complete, just as it is, and the Norio person's perspective, unique though it may be, is unimportant and without privilege. And in that recognition is contained a sense of sameness with the rest of humanity. The Norio person's sense of self has all but disappeared.

7

THE COSMIC
TWO-BY-FOUR

THE MIND AT REST MAY not be engaged in chatter, but it is also not inactive. It continues to recognize and realize. It does so with a faculty Norio calls insight. Insight, Norio says, is to be distinguished from ordinary thought. While thinking is a strictly cerebral affair, insight is whole-body, taking form in sensations and images before it is verbalized.

Much later, when he is invited to talk about his findings, Norio will explain the mechanisms of thought and insight in terms of a conceptual model. Our humanness, he proposes, is like an onion. It is built layer upon layer around a core. The onion-like construction's outermost layers are those given to thinking.

Thinking, especially the rational kind, is a uniquely human endeavor. By nature, it is linear: it relates cause to effect, much the way sentences relate subjects to predicates, and it builds upon itself, one thought leading to the next. It also comes in various flavors. Thinking can, for example, be logical, speculative, fanciful, or comic. And it thrives on relative distinctions, especially as pertain to values and qualities. Value distinctions are commonly made in terms of opposites, such as true or false, right or wrong, accurate or inaccurate, beautiful or ugly, and so on. Quality distinctions include high or low, bright or dark, bitter or sweet, red or blue or yellow; the list is endless.

Furthermore, as those distinctions would indicate, thought is invariably framed in language. The entire thinking enterprise is predicated on the mind's ability to generate abstractions from experience and then to name those abstractions, to give them verbal or written markers or symbols subject to grammatical manipulation. Yes, the mind also thinks in visual and auditory images. But not exclusively. It requires the symbolic logic and syntax of language to tie these images together and to make them meaningful.

Another feature of the thinking mind is its grounding in the notions of past, present, and future. It is grounded in psychological time. Norio's recognition of the fragility of that grounding was seminal to his discovery of the space between thoughts.

The next layers of the onion are, in many ways, antithetical to those above. They are given to feelings. Feelings are pre-rational. They are also non-linear, occurring spontaneously and intuitively. And they have no remembered past or imagined future; they show up only in the present. Some of these feelings—sensations of joy or love, for example—are innate. Others, such as the sorrow Norio inquired into during his drive across Nevada, are acquired so early on as to be held as part of the human package.

The case of sorrow deserves some further exposition. What Norio refers to as sorrow is a natural human response to separation. When we acquire the notion of a separate psychological self, we are reflexively given to nostalgia; we long for unity. Nostalgia translates into sorrow. And sorrow subsequently translates into other base feelings, including anger and fear.

The feelings being described here are to be distinguished from emotions. To see that distinction, it is important first to note that the names used in the preceding paragraph—joy, love, sorrow—only occur in our attempts to describe those feelings, while the feelings presence themselves unnamed. Just as Norio describes his moments of clarity and certainty as being preceded by a feeling, feelings are intuitive. They are also non-local. And they only occur when the body is relaxed.

Emotions, on the other hand, are part of the thinking self as well as the feeling one. They are the entanglement of feelings with thoughts. Physically, they are felt as tensions or constrictions within specific and isolated areas of the body, such as the area around the solar plexus or the chest. Most importantly, emotions assume causality. They take on the thinking self's habit of assigning cause, thus arriving at formulations such as, "I am sad (or happy) as a result of such-and-such an event or circumstance."

Silence, Norio sees, is the feeling and thinking layers' substratum. While perpetually mute and non-invasive, it is also ever present. It is causative, in the sense that the silent layer is what gives rise to the onion's feelings and thoughts. And it is in direct communication with the onion's core. The agent of that communication is energy, the energy that, Norio concludes, is the source of all knowing. It can also be characterized qualitatively as infinitely and unconditionally loving.

Then there is the core of the onion, whereof not much can be said, only because it falls outside the purview of words and language. In looking into that core, Norio sees—here, the words looking and sees are inadequate but will have to suffice—one, that it is singular and causal, that all onions share the same core, and that all that arises in the layers above is ultimately attributable to it. And, two, that it is infinite, without limit or constraint.

The Norio person, like all people, is representative of the complete package, the whole ball of wax. That realization is not to be held lightly, for it necessitates acceptance of all the onion's many facets. It means, for example, that silence, just because it is deeper within the onion and closer to source, is no more important to the onion's integrity than are thinking and feeling. After all, silence is only recognizable as "silence" in thinking. Silence is not the negation of thought but the enablement of it. Silence and thought are not two; they are two sides of a single coin.

Likewise, neither is thinking necessarily an obstruction to knowing the onion in its entirety, nor is the thinking mind necessarily the enemy of equanimity. Only when the thinking layers become divorced from the layers beneath them and take on a life of their own do they become a problem. A mind in communication

Silence → feeling → thought

with the onion's core is driven by the same energy that generates, first, silence and then, feeling. And when the thinking self rests, it naturally subsides first into the feeling self, then into silence, then into core. That trajectory is the one followed by Norio upon discovering the spaces between thoughts. It is also the one followed by each of us at night during sleep.

Thinking, then, in its natural and uninhibited form, is a whole-onion undertaking. But somewhere during human development, the mind has taken a wrong turn. It has begun to think about itself. The thinking mind thinking about itself constructs a false sense of importance, a false sense of autonomy, and a false sense of separation. It disassociates from the rest of the onion. And such disassociation can never end well. It results in mental anguish, despair, desire, enmity, and all the other ingredients of human misery.

Thoughts, when generated in a state of disassociation, have no basis in whole-onion being. They are no more than mental machinations, the devolution of inspiration into repetitious chatter. Thinking thus generated chases its own tail around circular pathways etched in the outermost layers of the onion and in the neurological fabric of the brain, while the mind, preoccupied with such circular patterns of thought, falls out of communication with the deeper layers of being. It acts less out of critical reasoning and more out of habit. Eventually, its habit-driven thought processes drown out silence and even the memory of silence.

Insight, on the other hand, occurs outside of such habit-driven thinking. As the word implies, it is a product of inward vision; that is, the onion looks to its own core to discover what is so. Whether the object of consideration is internal or external or abstract or concrete makes little difference, since the onion's core touches on the oneness of all phenomena. Insight apprehends the nature of things through affinity. What emerges from such affinity is framed in a visionary kind of logic independent of value and quality distinctions or formally logical thought processes. As opposed to being used by language—as is the incessant chattering of the disassociated mind—the insightful mind uses language to form thoughts capable of meaningful expression. Norio, having surrendered his thinking self to silence, is guided on his journey almost exclusively by insight.

The day after his entry into the great silence by way of the space between thoughts, Norio makes a run to Oklahoma. Two days later, he is back in Southern California.

On the morning of the fourth day, as he exits the freeway headed for his next pickup, he notices a sculpture-like rocky outcrop. This is one of those moments of insight. He sees not just the outward form and color of the rocks but their existential is-ness. Until now, he has thought of rocks only as staid and stationary parts of the landscape. They have no volition, they do not entertain, and they do not make good friends. What he is now seeing, however, is energetic entities. The rocks are suffused with energy. They are nothing but the crystallization of energy. In a certain sense, they are even alive.

Moreover, the energy in the rocks is the same energy permeating every other object within his field of vision. It is the same energy infused in the cells of his body. Whether manifesting in rocks or in humans, that energy knows just exactly what it is up to; it is intelligent beyond all measure, and it renders all complete. Which is to say, observer and observed are of the same stuff. Is there a Norio person looking at the rocks, or is there only a looking and a being seen? Aren't both the Norio person and the rocks perhaps functions of a single movement?

He continues his drive past warehouses and factories, ever less sure where he ends and the world begins. The Southern California landscape is simply occurring within a space of awareness. But who's awareness? Isn't Norio, the observer, also part of the world?

Then, just as he is approaching his destination, it hits him. If the all is a function of one intelligent energy, then the psychological entity Norio has no basis in what is real. It is made up. The Norio story, the Norio wants and desires, the Norio opinions and beliefs—all of these are delusions. They are fictions. There is no little man inside the machine.

"Oh, my God!" He is shocked out of silence just long enough to voice these words under his breath. They reverberate in every cell of his body. "There is no me. I don't exist!"

It's a rude awakening, a most radical realization. It's shattering. It's exhilarating. And it's wildly funny. It's the punchline to the cosmic joke: "The only thing in the way of me having everything I ever wanted is me." Norio is the only thing preventing Norio from seeing himself as whole and complete.

Part of the shock factor is being shown the depth of his own ignorance. Here he has been driving in a state of blissful silence for four days, never once inconvenienced by the absence of his thinking self. It has taken nothing away from his ability to operate within the domain of ordinary human affairs: he has never missed a turn, his driving has never interrupted traffic, and he has made all his deliveries on time. And yet, all along, he has assumed the existence of a "me," an owner of the little voice within. He has assumed that, during the silence, the me has only been on break; it has taken a holiday. But no. There is no "me." There never was. It's a concoction. "Me" is nothing but a thought. It has taken the universe to come crashing down on top of his head to wake him up. It has taken being hit over the head by the cosmic two-by-four.

Some sharpening of terms is in order. The dissolution of the psychological Norio most obviously does not mean the end of the Norio person. The Norio person is an entity, an individuated but holistic whole. It is an onion among onions. And onions have agency and structural unity. That agency and structural unity is sometimes called ego. The ego ensures that, when the onion picks up and walks across the room, it does so as a unit, that it doesn't leave any of its parts behind. Within contemporary spiritual and New Age circles, the ego has been given something of a bad rap; it's held accountable for the misdeeds Norio attributes to the false sense of self. But the ego in its essence is no more than the onion being an onion. It is necessary and fundamental to the onion's ability to function as an entity among other entities.

The mistake occurs when the ego is attributed with a psychology. While only one onion gets to see the world through Norio person eyes, the Norio doing the seeing is not a psychological Norio. This is obvious because the psychological Norio is an object of experience; through introspection, it can be seen in all its facets—its stories, its comedies and tragedies, its accomplishments and failures, its dreams and fears, and so on. Such seeing is indeed the very enterprise to which he has devoted his attention for the last year, his personal project. And that which is being seen cannot possibly be doing the seeing.

Where the ego is functionally real, the psychological self is a fiction. It is self-created, dreamt up by the mind. This is what Norio calls the separate self. It's the self that lives exclusively in the onion's thinking layers and experiences itself as isolated and incomplete. Which is why it is always seeking completion.

In the aftermath of his having been hit over the head with the cosmic two-by-four, Norio reflects upon what his life up until this point has looked like. What shows up is a particularly bad opera. He has been living, it seems, a mindless emotional drama put to insipid music. And when he thinks opera, he thinks phantom. "The Phantom of the Opera." His opera is one in which the leading role has been performed by a phantom self. Or more accurately, by a phantom self-ing, since the phantom is constantly reconstituting and reinforcing its persona. The opera thus exposed, what is revealed is the stage, the props, and the performance. It's simple entertainment. Moreover, what had been drama becomes pure and unadulterated comedy. How ridiculous that he should have been fooled into believing the opera's storyline. How could he have mistaken what is occurring on stage for actuality?

He also sees in the aftermath that what is left of Norio-ness is shared with the rest of humanity. He is no longer subject to Norio thoughts and emotions; he is subject to human thoughts and emotions. He is just one more example of human form experiencing life and the world in the way humans do. And given this new sense of connection, of commonality, he feels for the first time an imperative to share the cosmic joke and its punchline with family and friends, perhaps even with others.

What began as a personal project has become something else, something quite transpersonal. Yes, he has a unique identity, but the humanity of that identity takes precedence over its uniqueness. Even the lines between self and other begin to blur; he is seeing more and more of other in self and self in other. Given that humanity is evidently one, what could be more natural than to want to share the knowing that we, the human enterprise, are ever already whole and complete, that nothing is wanting, that we are right here right now living in heaven on earth?

Realistically, however, how do you look another person in the eye and tell them, "You don't exist"? He needs only to think about how unready he would have been just weeks ago to receive the same message. The task of formulating what he wants to say into a message that can be received and understood, even if only by those with ears to listen, is daunting. It is more difficult than anything else he has ever undertaken. And it continues to the present day.

For another ten days, the silence continues. It is pristine and crisp, almost crinkly in its clarity. Even when normal thinking returns, it is altered. First, thinking does not drown out the silence; the silence is always there and immediately available. Thoughts occur within the context of silence, or as silence in action. Second, his thinking is no longer strictly cerebral; it is whole-onion thinking, always in communication with the onion's core. It is fed by insight and insight's visionary logic.

Out of this thinking emerges a daydream, a metaphoric or symbolic representation of his recent journey. Even though it is imaginary, it occurs in such high definition as to feel substantive and real. In it, he is in a darkly lit room. That is, the daydreamer recognizes he is in a room, but the Norio in the dream does not. The Norio in the daydream sees only an intimately familiar world-space, the one he has grown up in and knows. Half-seeing, half-feeling, he gropes his way around within this space. The objects he encounters are also familiar; he recognizes them immediately through sight and touch.

Those objects, the daydreamer recognizes, are products of what he has learned and been taught since he was a child. They are culturally determined artifacts. A carpet is only a carpet in the context of a culturally determined lifestyle; a couch is only a couch when it is commonly recognized as an object upon which to sit. These objects are defined in terms of utility and purpose, and he is guided in his use of them almost entirely by habit.

The Norio in the dream is living not so much among real objects as among artifacts and ideas. He is living the map, not the territory.

Something, however, causes the dream Norio to question the nature of these habits. The path he has charted, using his map, only leads to more locations on the map; the known only leads to more of the known. Whereas life is a continuous journey into the unknown. Life, he sees, in a moment of insight, is not going to turn out. With this realization, he can no longer rely on the known, much less on representations of the known. He throws away the map.

When he does, he sees the room for the first time as a room. He sees it has four walls. How curious! He has been living inside a room, all the while thinking the space inside the room was all there is. The room, once dark, is now amply lit, even though he hasn't been near a light switch. His attention is drawn to the walls, and they come into focus. Where there are walls, there must be other rooms. Where there is an inside, there must be an outside.

And now, another surprise. In one of the walls is a window. The house does indeed have an outside. The window looks out onto a garden, and the garden is in full bloom. It almost shouts to him with color.

Just to the side of the window, he sees a door. It is the space between thoughts. He opens the door and steps out into the garden.

It's unlike any garden he has ever seen. The magnificence of the flowers and shrubs, the dancing sunlight and gentle breeze, the bees and humming birds; this is paradise! Tears of joy form in the corners of his eyes. The intensity of wonder and beauty is excruciating, as is the sense of privilege to witness such perfection.

The garden is immense. It encircles the entire house, making the house not an inside to the garden's outside but just one more feature of the garden. The house too is perfect and complete. It contains, he can tell now from the numerous windows and gables, many, many rooms. To the inhabitants of each of those rooms, the room that is their world-space is all there is. Somehow, through the course of its social and cultural development, humanity has constructed rooms with walls that divide. It has obscured the reality that all live together in one big house and that the house sits in paradise. He is seeing this not as a privileged observer removed from humanity but as a member of the same house-building, room-building enterprise. How humorous it all is!

He ambles aimlessly about the garden drinking of its colors and delights for what feels like an eternity but is actually three days, those first three days of silence during which he drove to Oklahoma and back. Life in the garden is complete. He is fulfilled, and nothing is wanting. That there could be something more than this garden doesn't even occur to him.

But then, on the morning of the fourth day, he comes upon a wall. Again, how curious! Even this garden, it seems, has boundaries. Even it is contained. Silence, he is seeing, occurs within an even greater context, and that context is boundless and infinite energy. Furthermore, that energy is intelligent. Meaning not that intelligence is a quality of the energy but that intelligence and the energy are one and the same. The perfection and beauty of the garden is a product of this energetic intelligence.

And now, there within the wall is a gate. The attraction is irresistible. "What, I wonder, is beyond the gate?" He opens the gate and steps through. He is hit over the head by the cosmic two-by-four.

On the other side of the gate is formless void, utter unknown. Nothing to see and nothing to hear, so nothing to describe. Furthermore, both the experiencer and the experienced are gone; no more observer and observed. What remains is a single movement. Call it experience. Call it observation. It is an awareness that has neither inside nor outside, no purpose and no cause. It comes out of nowhere and is moving toward nothing. It just flows. It flows without any trace of propulsion or effort. This flow, the awareness apprehends, is the essence of evolution.

Oddly, however, even though sense of self has vanished, a sense of entity, of individual integrity remains. The entity, the awareness intuits, is but one of an infinite number of similar entities all moving in a similar fashion into the unknown. Furthermore, the awareness also intuits that somewhere deep within that unknown, all the individual strands, all the infinite movements of experience, are being drawn into a singularity. All are being returned to source.

The awareness that is all that remains of Norio now turns around to look back in the direction from whence it has come. What had appeared to be a grand movement toward source now appears to be a grand movement out of source into creation and the world. That movement might be described as a river of energy or as an ocean that ebbs and flows. Not only is this energy the formal aspect of intelligence, but it is pure and unbridled potential. It is the essence of creativity. And it is the essence of love. It embraces all and holds all close to its heart. There is no escaping it, no sin that can be committed against it, no possibility of error or transgression.

The gate is gone, the garden is gone, the house is gone. Just as Norio, the observer, is gone, done in by the cosmic two-by-four. All have been but mirages, chimera. What opens before him instead is infinite possibility. He can become whatever and whomever he wants. Yet somehow, through myriad pathways with myriad forks, he settles on the Norio person. The unique vehicle through which he will experience life and the world is named Norio, and it drives a truck for a living.

When the Norio awareness steps through the gate, it holds a question. How is it the Norio person has allowed itself to be fooled for so long? Moreover, the question is not just of personal consequence. For how is it humanity allows itself to be fooled? How is it that mankind, for whom wholeness and equanimity are birthrights, consistently settles for a state of existence wherein misery and suffering are the rule?

The answer that is returned from the unknown is both obvious and surprising. The prerogative and ability to turn one's back on paradise comes through language. It occurs because we are linguistic creatures. The very capacity that is man's greatest asset, the ability to think linguistically and to create linguistically, is his undoing. It undoes because it allows him to create separation, to imagine that which is doing the thinking as something it is not.

As humans, the extent to which we are wedded to language escapes our notice. But think about it. What iota of our human world would or could exist but for language? Even in asking that question, are you not doing so, as well as framing your attempt to answer it, in language?

To state the claim more strongly, the human domain exists in and is constructed out of language. The depth of language's reach goes far beyond the obvious distinctions, such as laws and customs and mores and beliefs and so on. It includes even the most basic "facts" of our reality. It includes even the objects of our experience.

Take the tree in your yard, for example. The birds and the squirrels also recognize the tree. They may even make their homes in it. But only we recognize it as a "tree." Nor is that "tree" limited to the tree in your yard; for speakers of English, "tree" applies to species of arbor all over the world. It is representative of an extraordinary human ability to name abstractions and then to think and communicate using those names.

From the Norio entity's perspective, looking back at where the gate, garden, and house had once been and where all there is now is free-flowing energy, the faculty of language is nothing more than that energy made human. Humanity's ability to think and communicate in language is the embodiment of primordial intelligence and creativity in the thinking layers of the onion. Language does not just show up in thinking; it *is* thinking. Thinking is languaging. We, as individuals and as humanity, literally language ourselves into existence.

Herein the conundrum. For in languaging ourselves into existence, we don't do so willfully or even consciously. The linguistically constructed human

mind talking to itself using language

world is given to us at birth. Which is to say, we acquire it through learning, while that which is acquired is preexisting. We are thrown into it. We inherit it, replete with all its strengths and foibles.

If you are a native speaker of English, not only do you communicate in English, you also think in it. As much as you may wish to claim your thoughts as private and personal, they are occurring in a public medium. They are occurring in a cultural world space. You did not invent that world-space; you acquired it. And you acquired not just the words and grammar of English but the entire historical, social, and cultural habitat it invokes.

The cultural assumptions and social norms of the world-space we inhabit become part of the fabric of our being. In a world wherein most of humanity is asleep, however, these cultural assumptions and social norms are almost all founded upon mistaken identity. They assume separateness and impotence. They are tied to beliefs in either/or, win/lose, have/have not, eat/be eaten.

And this is the crux of the matter. For the self, you see, is constructed through language. The self is a conceptual creation. It is languaged into existence by a mind that does not know the power of language and that continually talks to itself. The separate self is just that and nothing more, the mind talking to itself. It is a

spider web

product of habit-driven languaging, every incidence of which reinforces the mistaken assumption that what the mind calls "me" is real and that observer and observed are separate.

In stepping outside of the mind and into silence, the Norio awareness was able to see language and languaging as a phenomenon. It was able to see that everything the mind had believed about itself, all the Norio stories it told itself, were linguistic creations. They were collections of words. Furthermore, they were words imbued with socially and culturally predetermined meanings rooted in relative values. And they were being used predominantly to reflect a dull and sordid human world based on assumptions of separation and mortality.

Moreover, the Norio awareness is empowered by silence to see even the self as a linguistic construction. The belief that the self is separate and finite is only a belief. And once awareness sees the separate self as a phantom of the mind's creation, it can never go back to the same lie. Furthermore, thus liberated from the constraints of mistaken identity, it is prompted to share this liberation with others. It is motivated to attempt to say what cannot be said, to challenge the limits of language.

8

First Talk

*Ben, the
carpenter*

ONE YEAR PRIOR TO HIS February 2005 encounter with
the cosmic two-by-four, Norio calls his friend Ben in
Maine. He makes the call a couple of weeks prior to the
one in which he tells Ben about his personal project and
how he is observing himself the way an entomologist
observes a butterfly.

Ben is a talented carpenter. He is also a talented
astrologer. Ben's astrological prowess is known only
among his friends, and he has never, ever charged for
his services. His readings can be uncannily perceptive.
To what extent he derives his information from the
positions of the planets as opposed to pure intuition,
even he is unsure. But when he looks at an astrological

chart and compares it with what is going on in the heavens at present, he sees things others don't. Norio and Ben have spoken about this ability. It seems to derive from the same sort of power of insight Norio has also experienced repeatedly—the difference being only that, for Ben, it's the planets and their aspects that act as a trigger.

"It's been a while since you've read my chart," Norio says. Twenty-five years, to be exact. Not that Norio is looking for advice; he has, after all, given up on living for a future. He's just curious. They set a date and a time, and several days later, at the appointed time, Norio calls again from a truck stop in Castaic, California, just outside Santa Clarita.

"I'd forgotten how interesting your chart is," Ben begins. "It's really clear you're here for a single purpose."

"Really? What is it?"

"You'll find out in the beginning of February 2005."

Ben continues. "You'll be giving talks. You'll be talking about what Krishnamurti talked about."

This is all news to Norio. "Who's Krishnamurti?" he asks.

During this same conversation, Ben also inquires, "How's your father's health?"

"Fine, as far as I know," Norio answers. "Why do you ask?"

"That's good to hear. He's most likely going to develop colon cancer over the next several months."

Norio takes Ben's warning to heart but without alarm. Prediction only becomes prediction after the fact; until then, it is just speculation. He says nothing to his father or brothers.

In June, however, he receives an email from his brother Phiya saying, "Dad is having some health problems. He is suffering abdominal pains."

In August he sees his father in Vermont at the annual macrobiotic summer camp and goes out to dinner with him and a small group of friends. Michio appears to be his usual self, but Norio notices he hardly touches his food.

Then in September, word comes that Michio has been rushed to the emergency room at Mount Auburn Hospital in Cambridge and been admitted. Norio, in Ohio, calls his dispatcher and explains the circumstances. The dispatcher finds a run that will take him to Boston, and Norio drives overnight, arriving the following morning. After his delivery, he parks his truck off Route 128 in Newton and has a friend pick him up. He is the first of the four Kushi brothers to reach the hospital: Hal arrives shortly after from New York; Hisao gets in the next day from California; and Phiya, the day after that, from western Massachusetts.

The doctors have no good news. They have removed a tumor that was completely blocking his colon. But the cancer has already spread, and there is not much more they can do. They estimate he has two weeks to a month left to live.

Norio is distressed. He calls Ben from the hospital parking lot.

"The doctors don't know what they're talking about," Ben tells him. "He'll be fine. He's going to live through this and continue living for at least another ten years."

Norio is consoled. Michio does indeed recover and lives for another ten years and three months, passing on December 28, 2014, at the age of eighty-eight.

As he did with the warning regarding his father's health, Norio holds the other parts of Ben's reading lightly. A singular purpose? Talks? Maybe so, maybe not. He will know when the time comes.

In January 2005, however, he mentions the reading to a friend in Asheville, North Carolina, named Courtney.

"Oh, well I can arrange a talk," she says. Norio plays along. He hasn't a clue what he is to talk about;

but then, February—when, supposedly, his purpose is to be revealed—has yet to come. The talk is set for March 1 in Asheville at the Indigenous Tea House.

March 1 arrives. No doubt now as to what he is to talk about. He is to tell his audience what it's like to be hit over the head with a cosmic two-by-four. He is to share the punchline to the cosmic joke.

The Norio person standing in front of the dozen people assembled is radically different from the one who agreed to this talk a month and a half ago. Just back from his two-week sabbatical in the silence of being, he is operating in a state of semi-euphoria, a sustained high. He is an awareness devoid of identity or history, and he has all but forgotten what it was like to have once been trapped inside a separate self and a personal story.

Norio has nothing riding on this talk and carries none of the weight associated with goals or expectations. He only wants to share what he sees. The fallacy of the separate self is so obvious. It is also the good news everyone is seeking. What he has to say is exactly what they have come to hear; of this, he is certain.

"We already have everything we could ever want," he begins. "We're already perfect, whole, and complete. The only thing in the way of seeing we are perfect, whole, and complete is ourselves. We are fooled by the illusion of a separate self."

He has said it. He has told them the punchline to the cosmic joke. But no one is laughing. The faces in the small audience are looking back at him without expression. They are looking at him as if he hasn't said anything yet. He has delivered his message in its entirety, and they're waiting for his talk to begin.

Norio, as he is no longer capable of taking anything personally, suffers no embarrassment or injury over the Indigenous Tea House debacle. But he does acknowledge that delivering the joke and its punchline in a way that people get it is going to be far more difficult than he had supposed.

Of course, people are not going to get the joke. Would he have gotten it had it been told to him even a month ago? What is now obvious to him is not necessarily obvious to others. Nor will simply saying it do the trick. Telling the punchline is not going to deliver the goods. How, then, is he to make his message make sense?

This puzzle begets a new project. He sets out to come up with a method to communicate what he sees regarding the human condition in a way that others will understand. In approaching this project, he reflects, "Surely I'm not the only one to have seen this. There must be others who have seen it too. What are they saying? And how are they saying it?"

It's a field about which he knows nothing, so he asks around among friends. One such friend gives him *The Power of Now*, by Eckhart Tolle. When he visits me in Richmond, I give him my copy of *The Awakening of Intelligence*, by Jiddu Krishnamurti, the name he first heard from Ben. Yet another friend sends him a DVD of a talk by Adyashanti. All of these, he absorbs. Yes, indeed, others have arrived at similar realizations, and they have left behind an entire literature documenting and describing those realizations.

In earlier years, when he was still chasing success and seeking solutions to his problems, Norio would sometimes visit Barnes & Nobles and go straight to the "Self-help" section. He would look to see what was new and of interest in the field of self-development. Now, however, disabused of the notion of a self to develop, he has no use for self-help. He turns instead to the "Spirituality and New Age" section. Most of what he finds there—not to disparage it, for it is undoubtedly of interest and use to others—isn't pertinent to his project. But occasionally he will come across a hidden gem, and when he does, he looks to find who is the author, what is his or her message, and how is he or she communicating it.

One take-away from these writers is the usefulness of story. This comes as a surprise. He is not his story and has no interest in seeking to explain the present by way of the past. Story is but one more fiction invented by the separate self. But it is also a useful vehicle, he now recognizes, for talking about the human condition. Story communicates in ways that straightforward explanation can't. It helps to contextualize his thoughts and insights, and it helps to demonstrate and give meaning to ideas that are otherwise just abstractions.

He chooses, as the starting point for his narrative, the realization that life is not going to turn out. The choice, he acknowledges, is arbitrary; his story has no true beginning. But life not turning out, the marker for his giving up on living for a future, is convenient to his purpose.

He also sees the need for conceptual tools. He sets about inventing models or metaphors to demonstrate the ideas he wants to convey. The onion is such a model; the house, garden, and gate is another.

Finally, he invents exercises and step-by-step processes through which he can guide his audiences and call their attention to inconsistencies in their beliefs. Humanity's problems come not from the innocent ignorance of not knowing but from the self-indulgent ignorance of thinking we know what we don't. The mind typically takes itself as a given. It seeks answers from its environment, rarely suspecting its own limits and misconceptions as the root of its perplexity. But the mind is also not hopelessly intransigent. It sees its limits and misconceptions when shown.

These elements—story, model, and process—loosely combine to make up what Norio calls Norio nonsense. Even today, twelve years later, Norio nonsense is a work in progress. It's the sort of work that will never be complete.

If his first talk is a setback, his presence at that talk nevertheless shines through. What he is attempting to say, no one understands; but that he has something of value to say is eminently clear. Here and there and from time to time, other opportunities present themselves. Each of these becomes a source of invaluable feedback, informing him as to what works and what doesn't and giving him further ideas about what to say and how better to say it. His Norio nonsense has gradually gained exposure across a variety of mediums, including talks at gatherings and retreats, day-long seminars, conference call discussion groups, print media, and online interviews.

Shortly after emerging from his two-week sequester, Norio talks with JoAnne, as he does from time to time, by phone. They discuss the kids and the state of the household. And as usual, JoAnne has much more to say than he does.

As she is talking, she stops suddenly, mid-sentence, and says, "You're listening!" Norio laughs. JoAnne continues, then stops a second time. "I can't believe it. You're really listening!"

This time, Norio's laugh is robust and sustained. Yes, she is right. He hasn't been a good listener. Up until now, has he ever really listened to what she has had to say?

By a curious quirk of the English language, the words silent and listen spell themselves with the same six letters but in a different order. Without silence, can there be any listening? And can there be silence without someone to "listen" it?

The mind, however, has a habit of bringing its own agenda to every conversation. It filters the words of others through the prism of its own thoughts, opinions, and beliefs. Above all, it wants to be heard much more than it wants to listen. Match two minds similarly disposed, and you have a formula for disaster; the parties talk at and past each other. The wonder is that anything gets communicated at all. Given how rarely true listening occurs, should we expect human affairs to be in anything but a state of turmoil?

Relationship is fundamental to our existence. Even birth is a consequence of a specific relationship, and every child thus born is immediately and already related to a mother, a father and family, and a society. How odd, then, that we behave the way we do. Each of us operates as a walking, talking, sound machine impervious to the perspectives of others. Our conversations are all but predetermined by the opinions, positions, intentions, and expectations we bring to them, and our definitions of agreement and disagreement are based not on mutual concern for what is so but on confluence or disparity between our respective interests.

Norio notices he is seeing people in a different light. He no longer perceives anyone to be a stranger but feels an immediate familiarity, even intimacy, with the people he meets. What has shifted is the Norio person doing the meeting. Heretofore, interactions with others have always been tainted with danger. A self that is subject to hurt must protect itself; it must not allow too many openings. It must also be on the lookout for opportunities of advantage and seize those opportunities when they present themselves. Such a self goes around armed. It carries a sword and a shield.

Having given up the illusion of self, he has nothing to advance or protect, no need for either sword or shield. Furthermore, the magic of relationship becomes

I, and thou

palpable. When two or more come together, whether in conversation, in joint endeavor, or even in competition or open conflict, a communal space of relatedness emerges. This space is always novel and infused with potential. The individuals may carry forward into that space their respective histories, including their respective histories with each other, but the encounter is always a fresh start; and it is always larger, deeper, and more complex than what was there before.

Norio and JoAnne met in 1983. They were together for nine years before splitting in 2002. Despite their separation, they remained on good terms and in communication. For the Norio person, this is a habit of character: since long before his encounter with the cosmic two-by-four, he has remained in communication with every one of his past wives and girlfriends. But in JoAnne's case, the welfare of their children made such communication imperative. JoAnne also worked, but Norio continued to contribute the lion's share of the household income.

Both have been in and out of other relationships since their separation. The summer of 2011, however, found them both single and attending JoAnne's mother's family reunion in Florida. Nine years after separating, they came back together and have remained together since.

Norio's oldest, daughter Lianna, now married, gave birth to his first grandchild on the day of the solar eclipse in August 2017. His youngest, son Paul, has just spent his 2017–2018 junior college year studying in Japan.

9

NORIO NONSENSE

EACH ONION HAS ITS OWN unique perspective on the world, so no two worldviews are ever the same. Furthermore, as Norio discovered, one onion cannot possibly communicate its worldview in its entirety to another. The most it can do is point.

And pointing, as Norio also discovered, is where the rubber meets the road. Sharing what one sees is perhaps the most difficult part of being human. In Norio's case, since what he is pointing to is the non-duality of objectivity and subjectivity, the method of pointing doesn't fit within the realms of either science or religion. It falls somewhere within the realm of art.

What uniqueness of perspective does not imply, however, is that all of reality is relative, or that every onion is entitled to its own version of the truth. Truth and reality, by definition, must have validity for multiple observers. They are trans-onion. Nevertheless, interpretations of truth, as well as expressions of those interpretations, do vary and vary widely. Descriptions of the world are at least as numerous and various as the onions that espouse them.

Furthermore—and this is the crux of the human predicament—descriptions of the world are social constructions as well as individual ones. Onions, by nature, are social entities. They are connected, we might say, by the subliminal memory that they share the same core. And consequently, what one onion thinks or says affects all other onions. Social responsibility is implicit to the human domain.

The separation of self from the commonality at the core of human being is ultimately, as we have seen, a function of human languaging. It is a collective construct that has been cultivated and has persisted since the earliest beginnings of our historical memory. So deeply embedded in the human fabric is it that it passes for objective truth.

We are born into this construct. Or perhaps more accurately, we are born out of it. It imparts its cumulative assumptions, biases, and beliefs. We acquire these as we do other givens, such as the rising and setting of the sun, the blueness of the sky, and so on. Social and cultural conventions are as real to us as the earth, sky, and sea.

And yet, much of what we believe to be fact just doesn't hold up under scrutiny. This is especially so in the context of this modern, rational, scientifically oriented world, where the concept of universe as holographic enterprise, the parts of which reflect the order and evolutionary imperative of the whole, is gaining ever more traction. Does it make any sense whatsoever to suppose that I alone stand apart from the universe? That the I inside me is anything less than a direct reflection of the whole? That the I is of a stuff other than the singularity out of which all this evidently emerged? Is it not possible, even likely, that the I to which each of us so intransigently lays claim is a single being-ness assuming a multiplicity of unique perspectives?

Herein the great contradiction and the cosmic joke. When we wake up to the fallacy of the separate self, just who is it that wakes up? Certainly not the separate self, for that goes poof, up in smoke, the moment it is exposed. It's also not the timeless "I am" awareness, for that is ever already awake. So, who is it?

Consider the possibility that non-dual awareness is not something to be attained or woken up into, but that it already is. That the notions of separation, mortality, and sorrow are just ideas that have inserted themselves into our minds.

The mind isn't a thing. Or at least, if it is, no one has ever found it, despite all the scrutiny given to the brain. "Mind" we understand as a label for a collection of processes occurring in the brain. It is also our subjective experience of those processes. We can describe it as the virtual container within which thinking occurs.

Thinking is a form of action, of mental doing, the exercising of the mind. And given that this exercising of the mind is what most of us identify with most of the time, isn't it something of a misnomer to refer to ourselves as human beings? Aren't we really human doings?

Being, as opposed to doing, isn't a capacity of the mind. Nor is it something the mind can comprehend because it's not an object of experience. Mind can think about and attempt to describe being, but it can't know what it is to be. Descriptions and explanations are doings, and anything we say about being is prone to conceal more than it reveals. Even speaking about being and doing in the same sentence, as if one is the antithesis of the other, is a problem. Being is not antithetical to anything. It's the condition of universal singularity as expressed within the individual but holistic entities we're calling onions. Whereas mind, on the other hand, is a conceptual construct delivered up by the same collection of mental processes the word mind signifies. Mind ascribes to itself all manner of attributes, including autonomy and volition, but aren't those attributes just more of the same mental doing? Mind is but a thought.

Suppose you've lost your car keys. What do you do?

This is a problem the mind is well equipped to handle. It thinks back to where you were when you last had the keys in your hand and then retraces your steps from then until now. Did you put them down somewhere? Or did they slip out of your pocket when you were sitting in that armchair or on that sofa? While you are looking for your car keys, your mind holds the image of what the keys look like so that you can recognize them when you eventually find them.

Compare this with the search for awakening or enlightenment. This is a task for which the mind is not only not equipped but is a hindrance.

Just look, to begin with, at how the mind frames the problem. It is looking for "awakening" and/or "enlightenment" as if they are car keys, as if they are objects. Furthermore, who or what is it that's doing the looking? Isn't it the mind? And doesn't that make the whole search a sleeveless errand? Because what we can know with the mind is, awakening and enlightenment are not of the mind and are unknowable by the mind. Seeking awakening or enlightenment is a bit like searching for the car keys you never lost.

There is, however, a way of seeing and knowing that is not of the mind. Intuitively, we all know this to be so. Otherwise how is it we know what we know? And I don't mean rote learning but the kind of knowing that says, "Oh, that's what he's saying! That's what he means by insight!" It's the "Ah ha!" moment wherein objective and subjective collapse into a single perspective. When it occurs, the you to whom it occurs is forever changed. Before, the you didn't understand; now it does.

Looking for awakening or enlightenment either from memory or from conceptual understanding derived from what you have read or heard is a non-starter. It's an adult version of looking for Santa Claus. Should the mind find "awakening" or "enlightenment," we can be sure that what it has found is neither awakening nor enlightenment. The looking, to be effective, must come from other than mind. It must not be a seeking, for seeking implies a premonition or expectation of something to be found. The only purpose of looking is to see what is so.

And one thing that is so is, there's no such thing as awakening or enlightenment as conceived by the mind.

When asked about awakening or enlightenment, Norio usually professes ignorance. "I have no idea if I'm awake or enlightened," he will say. These terms did not become part of his vocabulary until after he began sharing his story, including that of being hit over the head with the cosmic two-by-four.

"Are you enlightened?" a woman at one of his talks asked. He didn't know what she meant. Through his readings, and through conversations with others, he has since learned the meanings of enlightenment and awakening, but he has never owned them.

For one thing, they smell of elitism. They imply there are those who are awake or enlightened and those who are not, and that those who are, are exceptional. The awakened ones belong to an order of avatars chosen to play a special role in the evolution of humanity. Having transcended the mundane, they are to serve, from seats in a higher dimension, as our guides.

For another, awakening and enlightenment are construed to be legitimate goals of spiritual practice. From the Buddha's story forward, liberation has been described as a culmination of arduous seeking and asceticism. It's the carrot tied to the end of the stick, the just reward for virtuous and pious devotion.

Norio has nothing to say about meditation or other kinds of spiritual practice since he has no experience with them. He is here to say, however, that if those practices are necessary to the achievement of awakening or enlightenment, then what he is pointing to is not awakening or enlightenment. What he wishes others to see is the most mundane and the most real, that which is so. Far from special, it's eminently plain and common, ever already present. Access to present reality requires no effort, no discipline, no price of admission. What's real is all there is. Rather than a goal to be coveted, it's the baseline of human existence, the "what is" from which living begins. Neither an aberration nor a privilege meted out to the few, if it's accessible to him, then it's accessible to everyone. It is how we are designed to be.

When I look at the world through my eyes, I cannot see my face. In the same way, to the extent awareness is coming to the world through the eyes of a phantom self, it is incapable of distinguishing the phantom from what is real. What it can do, however, is distinguish the symptoms of phantom self-ing. And the underlying condition of those symptoms is fear.

Phantom self => fear

The phantom self, because it is a fiction, is inherently vulnerable. It lives in continual fear of being exposed for the fraud that it is. And because its survival depends upon that fraud's continuity, it lives for a future. It lives in a combination of apprehension and expectation. Without coming completely to terms with what is, it lives for what's next. It avoids the emptiness that is the essential nature of its being by throwing itself into the work of becoming. Against all odds, it continuously strives to become real. *Creates challenges => solves them*

One tactic adopted by the phantom self as it strives to become real is to create challenges and problems. Challenges and problems are the phantom self-ing's way of reaffirming its central importance to the narrative it is choosing to live. It finds meaning and purpose in overcoming the challenges with which it confronts itself.

Because the phantom self-ing imagines itself as an entity separate from the world, its relationship with the world—with its environment, its circumstances, its promises and commitments, and other phantom selves— is fundamentally confrontational. It's a dangerous world out there, but a self's gotta do what a self's gotta do. It approaches life as a warrior approaches battle, ever on the lookout for enemies and ever ready to defend itself. It goes through life armed with sword and shield.

Relationships, therefore, are construed to be fundamentally adversarial. The warrior needs to be careful not to let his vulnerabilities show. He values his relationships with other phantom selves based on utility and potential gain, and his interactions with them are strategically engineered; they are delivered with the intention of producing effects. Consciously or unconsciously, they are manipulative.

Manipulative strategies become part of the self's repertoire from a young age. For example, the child learns early on that its weakness and defenselessness is also its greatest strength, that if it cries loud enough and for long enough it will usually get what it wants. A little later, while interacting with its peers, it may learn to take the opposite approach, to flex its muscles and bully its way to results. Most of us retain some versions of these strategies long past childhood. Sometimes we play the crybaby, enacting weakness in the face of circumstances to pry sympathy from others. Sometimes we play the bully, asserting the priority of our needs and desires over competing needs and desires.

Over the years, most of us have refined our tactics to high degrees of sensitivity. We have learned how to be covert. We know when to feign sympathy or interest or admiration. And we know when to compromise. But all these tactics are executed out of self-interest; all are designed to get for ourselves the best deal possible. Even agreement we understand to be that state in which the respective interests of the parties are accommodated and aligned.

The underlying fear of the phantom self in human affairs is annihilation. It most fears what it knows subliminally to be true: it doesn't exist.

Just think what the consequences might be were the phantom self to admit its insubstantiality. It would need to give up its elitist claims; it would no longer be special or stand out from the crowd. Furthermore, it would lose its detachment. It would no longer be able to assert its impartiality, its status as the observer who gets to assess, evaluate, and interpret the world but to whom those assessments, evaluations, and interpretations do not apply.

It would need to relinquish its falsely conceived capacity to make decisions, its belief that it creates its future through the choices it makes. All this is predicated on the concept of a doer separate from but operating on its circumstances within a linear progression of events. As Norio discovered behind the wheel of his truck, take away the doer and its future, and what needs doing just gets done.

Moreover, it would no longer be capable of relating to fellow onions as separate selves. It would not depend upon validation from those onions for the maintenance of its sense of self-worth. And it would no longer approach those relationships as means to validation or gain, as means of getting what it wants.

Several years ago, a lady-friend confessed to Norio that she enjoyed being with him because he never judged her. The admission came from left field and caught him by surprise.

"There's nothing to judge," he told her.

Consider what relatedness might look like were it not based on false self-image and devoid of calculations concerning gain and loss. The space of relationship is always greater than the sum of its parts. Remove the blinders imposed by "personal" expectations and "personal" interests, and what remains can only be called miraculous.

We do our thinking in language. Not exclusively, of course; images and memories play their parts. But language is what holds the whole process together. Without language, whatever it is we are doing would not be called thinking.

If you are a native speaker of English, then you think in English. Isn't this odd? Why is it we think the way we talk? Who is it we're talking to when we think?

To ask the question another way, if the thinking we do occurs in a shared cultural medium, then to whom do those thoughts belong? Each of us eagerly claims ownership of what we think, but deconstruct those thoughts and what you get is a collection of vernacular words and phrases. Were other speakers of English able to eavesdrop on our thoughts, they would have no trouble following them. They might even resonate with them or recognize them as similar to their own.

Are we really the authors of our thoughts? How can we be so sure anything we think is truly original?

Language does not just communicate meaning through the manipulation of symbolic artifacts; it creates a world-space. The thinking you do has meaning only because the words you use have meaning within the English-speaking world. For those of us born into English linguistic environments, admission is free; we acquire language effortlessly as children. For those coming to the language from other language environments, there may be some work involved. But either way, a fluency in English licenses us to operate within a shared milieu, a platform of interdependent ideas and meanings constructed through cultural conditioning.

And among those ideas is that of a self. Remember back to earliest childhood. Most of us have no memory of what it was like before we began to talk. Which is to say, before the seeds of "I" as a psychological entity first began to take hold. (It's not that there is no memory before the birth of the I—we know from psychology that there is. But those memories simply don't show up as "my" memories because they have no self to attach themselves to.)

Through adolescence, the I becomes ever more nuanced and robust. It acquires character traits, abilities, strengths, and weaknesses. (These may derive from features of the onion's hard-wiring, but they only show up as "character traits," "abilities," "strengths," and "weaknesses" when claimed by the I.)

None of this is good or bad; it is just as it is. But it is important to recognize that all this occurs through the medium of language. "I" grows out of language.

As English speakers, we each refer to ourselves as "I." When we learn to write, we discover it to be one of the shortest words in the language, a single letter, the ninth in the alphabet, standing straight and tall. We each claim ownership of this letter I as the marker for an identity that is different from you and we and he and she and they.

The wonder of it is, we're all going around calling ourselves by the same name! "I" isn't unique to any of us. It's common to all. Given this is so, consider the possibility that the referent of I, that to which it is pointing, is also common to all. Consider the possibility that self is a universal aspect of humanity—perhaps even of all living species—and that individuality, that which distinguishes one individual from another, is the portal to that universal reservoir of self. Were that so, there would be no good selves or bad ones, no smart selves or stupid ones, no privileged selves or unprivileged ones, no worthy selves or unworthy ones, and so on. There would be no self to defend or protect. Nor would there be a self to be lonely or to suffer. The self would be our affinity for humanity and the source of our compassion. It would also answer our questions regarding mortality, for such a self would never die.

One of the objections often surfaced in response to Norio's nonsense is, isn't what you're selling a copout? Aren't you using "I don't exist" as an excuse to deny responsibility for your actions? You may be driving around in your truck in a state of bliss, but meanwhile the world is going to hell in a handbasket. What kind of answer to the pain and suffering of the world is it to say, "I don't exist"?

Another variation of this same objection goes, "I feel strongly about... [insert climate change, desecration of the environment, money in politics, the income gap, or whatever suites you]. You're telling me that's just a belief. But the problem is real. It's going to take a lot more than Norio nonsense to get me to put down my convictions and roll over to the tune of injustice."

That the innocent ramblings of a truck driver should elicit such strong reactions is, in and of itself, informative. But the objections also say more about the listening into which he is speaking than about the merits of what he is attempting to communicate. The listening is that of critical judgment. Anyone whose beliefs are challenged will be careful, perhaps even protective, of those beliefs; this is only natural. Furthermore, such objections are usually motivated by genuine concerns.

Norio nonsense has no bone to pick with concern for humanity or the future of the planet. When the bubble in which the separate self resides is burst, the individual thus laid bare feels the pain of humanity more acutely than ever. It cannot help but do so, for it *is* humanity. When a friend or family members dies, it feels sad. When it sees images of refugees adrift in the Mediterranean, it feels agony. It also sympathizes with the social and economic stress suffered by the people of those countries good enough to take the refugees in. And when it hears about oil spills, deforestation, and species extinction due to industrialization and urban sprawl, it experiences outrage.

Where it can, it takes appropriate action. It isn't averse to speaking out on social, political, economic, and environmental causes. The difference is, it also isn't invested in these actions. It isn't attached to outcomes. It acts selflessly—that is, in the absence of self.

It also acts out of a knowing that the world, including all its pain and sorrow and suffering, is ever already the great perfection. The world can never be incomplete, but it can become more complete. There are no wrongs to be righted, just rights to be made more right. And the only way to realize more completeness and rightness in the world is to come from a space of equanimity and absolute completion.

One time, when Norio was six, George Ohsawa came to visit. During his visit, he delivered a series of lectures in the Kushis' living room, and Norio listened in. The lectures were too much for him to follow in their entirety, but two things Ohsawa said stayed with him. The first was that, ultimately, there is only one human disease, that of arrogance. The second was that each

of us is responsible for everything that happens, even events on the far side of the world.

These assertions challenged Norio's young mind. He heard them as riddles. He didn't know yet what the word arrogance meant, but the idea that all disease should have a single cause was intriguing. And what was he to make of the notion that he, Norio, was responsible for what was happening in India and China? For several weeks afterwards, he grappled with these ideas, wondering incessantly how it could be that he was responsible for everything that happened. Even into his teens and early twenties, when something unexpected occurred, he would ask himself, "How am I responsible?"

Several years after he was hit over the head with the cosmic two-by-four, Norio reflected again on Ohsawa's words. Both claims now made perfect sense. Arrogance is but another name for the condition of belief in a separate self; it's the self-assertion of importance and exceptionalism. Take away the separation of self from the universe and you remove the dis-ease associated with physical malady. You also allow providence to take over. (Which, incidentally, is not an argument to refuse medical treatment when such treatment is appropriate; this too is providence.)

Responsibility is an outlook on the world. When what is looking is a separate self, the limits of its responsibility are determined by how big it thinks it is—whether that is impotently small, sensibly ordinary, or megalomaniacally large. Whereas the emptiness that remains when the illusion of self disappears is infinite and bottomless to an extent that accommodates the whole world. The I who is responsible is the world.

So, Norio realizes, this is what Ohsawa meant when he called his practical philosophy macrobiotics, "the great life." Ohsawa, after all, was but one onion attempting to communicate his vision to other onions, and such attempts are inevitably subject to both successes and failures. One of the pitfalls of macrobiotics is the propensity of its practitioners to equate yin and yang with cause and effect—to think, "because yin, therefore yang." But that was not what Ohsawa was saying. He was saying yin and yang are ever already in a state of balance and that nothing needs to be done to right the balance of the world. The paradox is, only in realizing this is man able to take responsibility for his life, including his health, and for the state of the world. While Norio never so intended, he finds himself, in espousing his nonsense, also carrying on George Ohsawa's tradition and the work of his father and mother. This too is part of the cosmic joke.

10

THE CONVERSATION

FROM EARLY ON IN HIS fascination with modes of wheeled transportation, Norio has seen the highway in front of him as the highway of life. What changed when he discovered that the highway and the driver were both but parts of a single movement was that the journey ceased to be personal. All the traffic on the road showed up as part of the same single flow, and all the drivers, as aspects of a single awareness. Truck driving ceased to be a personal vocation. It became instead but a tiny thread in the greater fabric of the human social infrastructure.

Furthermore, since life, it appears, is a universal phenomenon, to say life is a journey is to say that the universe itself is embarked on a journey, one of self-discovery.

To adequately parse the nature of life's journey, a couple of additional remarks are in order. First, the universe, because it is a big place, is unknowable in its entirety. When we say the universe is big, we are invoking more than the grandiosity of its physical dimensions—its length, width, depth, and duration. To borrow loosely from Ken Wilber's integral philosophy, we are also invoking its developmental topography as carved out by the impetus of evolution. The universe is made up of perspectives, each claiming a unique, multidimensional cosmic address, and the number of those perspectives is infinite. And since this is so, the universe that is seeking to discover itself through the phenomenon of life can never, ever know all of itself for all time. Which is to say, the journey of the phenomenon of life has no endpoint. In both human and universal terms, the end of living for a future also means the end of predetermination. We can rest assured that life will always bring up something new.

Second, the journey of self-discovery is not confined to—and I borrow again from integral philosophy—the "I-space" of the individual onion. It's also a function of the "we-space" brought forth through contact between two or more onions. Norio calls this the space of creativity, because it's the space that brings forth novelty and meaning. It's the space of communication.

Communication is more than that which occurs through verbal exchange. We communicate not just with our minds but with our hearts and our bodies and our being. Communication is vibratory, and because it is vibratory, it is subject to both dissonance and harmony.

I repeat. Communication includes more than verbal exchange. But then, it's also not other than verbal exchange. There may come a time in human evolution when verbal communication is no longer necessary, when we are able to communicate whole thoughts or feelings directly from mind to mind or from heart to heart. We can only speculate. What we can say with certainty, however, is, we ain't there yet.

Another way of saying this is, our humanity is a conversation. That which sets us most apart from all the other kinds of onions that inhabit this universe is our ability to frame our thoughts in words and sentences, to communicate them verbally, to write them down so they can have reach and duration beyond that of our individual voices, and to create human history, culture, and civilization. And all this is occurring not just in our individual interiors but also in the public discourse. Our humanity and its evolution are a collective endeavor.

Words are powerful. They have the power, after all, to create history, culture, and civilization. But let us not forget that it is the collective "we" who has imbued them with that power. Think about it. Everything that is "right" or "wrong" with the world, everything that is "good" or "bad," "desirable" or "undesirable," of "benefit" or "hindrance," and so on—all these are so because they are so framed in the human conversation. They are so framed by the words we use to describe them.

Words are powerful. But to what extent are we living at the effect of that power, and to what extent are we dispensing it? To what extent are we functioning under the spell of the words we use, and to what extent are we using them creatively, to serve the evolutionary mandate and to realize heaven on earth?

It's high time we awaken to the profundity of our humanity and realize we are who we are because we say so. It's time because such realization is evolution at work, and because we owe it to the universe and its imperative to discover itself. Moreover, this is a question of more than individual responsibility. Waking up only becomes an evolutionary advance when it gains we-space traction and asserts itself as a morphogenetic meme. Awakening is a collective endeavor. And the time for that endeavor is now.

The day Norio Kushi was hit over the head by the cosmic two-by-four, he relinquished all prior claim to knowledge or privilege and accepted that what he knew was he knew nothing. He was shown that he didn't know who he was. And without knowing who he was, how could he possibly know anything about the world? But in that realization of the extent of his ignorance, he also discovered freedom— freedom from worry, concern, suffering, and sorrow. If ignorance is bliss, then, it turns out, absolute ignorance is absolute bliss.

Knowing nothing is freeing because it means having everything to learn. It also liberates us from preconceived and socially imposed notions of what is possible. When the mind gives up on knowing, it can rest in the potential that is the future. There is a difference between living for a future and living for a present that has a future. Which is to say, the future, like the past, is a feature of the present, but the future, unlike the past, presents itself as a potential. It is a potential precisely because it is beholden to the present; it is beholden to what is so.

Thus, for example, for pigs to sprout wings may be a possibility, but it isn't a potentiality. The name given to mental conditions wherein improbable interpretations of reality are given credence is psychosis. Psychosis has also been defined as doing the same thing over and over while each time expecting a different result. That the same definition also seems to describe much of human history is less than comforting.

The limitations placed by conventional wisdom on our future are the most pernicious form of ignorance. Through unconscious languaging of itself into existence, humanity has engineered daunting barriers to its own evolution. It has decided just what it is capable of, and this is nothing short of mass psychosis. Who is to say humanity is incapable of meeting the challenges to our survival posed by nuclear arsenals, global climate change, economic and political instability? Lasting resolution of these and other problems are not the equivalent of pigs sprouting wings.

To reiterate, the measure of what is potentially possible is not personal belief. It is collective knowing. The next step in human evolution involves waking up collectively to the reality of the potential that we are. And as those who have eyes to see will recognize, this is a project already underway. The sort of awakening Norio describes is occurring with accelerating frequency among people living here and there around the globe. These awakenings carry the potential that is the future. The forward thrust into novelty that is evolution is gaining collective momentum and is searching for the critical mass that will declare this potentiality an eventuality.

In case you haven't figured it out yet, this book is not about answers. It's a book about questions. The reason for that is, life and the universe do not reveal themselves to us through answers. They reveal themselves through questions. Life is and always will be a mystery. But to accept that such is the case is not an invitation to throw in the towel on knowing. Quite the opposite. For it's in the discovery of the depth of our ignorance and the extent of our not knowing that life asserts its vitality. The journey of life is also an art, and a large part of that art is learning how to ask the right questions.

Norio's story is unique, and as a result, hopefully, it has made for a good read. But ultimately—as Norio will be the first to say—it's only a story. It may be entertaining, but it has no intrinsic importance. It's certainly not worthy of emulation, nor is it a recipe for self-discovery; we don't recommend you stop what you are doing and take up driving a truck. Our purpose in telling his story is to contribute some small nudge in the direction of global evolution and the realization of the potential that is now. Just what is the future of humanity is for none of us to say. What we can say with absolute certainty, however, is that awakening is both a personal responsibility and a global imperative, and that the time for its realization is at hand.

To Learn More...

For more information regarding this book, including news and updates, visit **awake-at-the-wheel.com**.

 If you have questions for Norio or are interested in hosting him as a speaker at an event or gathering, please email him at **norio@awake-at-the-wheel.com**.

To learn more about Stephen Earle and his other books and writings, visit **www.stephenearle.com**. You may also contact him by email at **steve@awake-at-the-wheel.com**.

For more great books visit Tatfoundation.org

Only the Real
Self has fear

& egoistic
thought

Love and
compass

↓

make you

strong

NO
EGO

↓

insight

dawns

insightful
dawns love
& compa

time
Present

Ego mind → Past → Pret → futu

Ego experiences → extremes

good bad lik dislik

Made in the USA
Middletown, DE
23 August 2019